Anonymous

**Manual of the Laws and Discipline of the Methodist Church in Ireland**

Anonymous

**Manual of the Laws and Discipline of the Methodist Church in Ireland**

ISBN/EAN: 9783337000356

Printed in Europe, USA, Canada, Australia, Japan

Cover: Foto ©Lupo / pixelio.de

More available books at **www.hansebooks.com**

# MANUAL

OF THE

# LAWS AND DISCIPLINE

OF THE

## Methodist Church in Ireland

Published by order of the Irish Conference,

## 1889.

Dublin:
PRINTED BY R. T. WHITE, 45 FLEET STREET.

1890.

# EDITORIAL NOTE.

The Editorial Committee appointed by the Conference to superintend the publication of the "Manual of Laws and Discipline" has found it necessary, in a few instances, for the sake of order and clearness, to alter the arrangement of the matter embraced in some of the Chapters; some Sections and paragraphs have also been recast with the same object.

In the progress of the work it was found that some matters of administration which by usage had become accepted "Rules" had not been formulated in any specific "Resolution" or "Minute"; these the Committee thought it within its function to put into *form*, and accordingly this has been done.

In no instance has any alteration in, or addition to, the undoubted "Rule" of the Connexion been attempted; and in any verbal changes which have been necessary in order to harmonize modes of expression, the Committee has been careful to maintain the spirit and intent of the original "Minute."

The arrangement of the whole subject matter in consecutively numbered paragraphs, facilitating, as it does, ready reference, will, it is hoped, be accepted as an improvement.

# CONTENTS.

## PART I.

## CONSTITUTION AND GOVERNMENT.

### CHAPTER I.
### ORIGIN OF METHODISM.

PAGE 1

### CHAPTER II.
### MEMBERS.

| | | PAGE |
|---|---|---|
| I. | Admission of Members | 7 |
| II. | Removal of Members | 7 |
| III. | On Conformity to the World | 8 |
| IV. | Bankruptcy of Members | 9 |
| V. | Marriage of Members | 10 |
| VI. | Observance of the Lord's Day | 10 |
| VII. | Support of the Ministry | 11 |
| VIII. | Trial and Exclusion of Members, | 12 |

### CHAPTER III.
### THE MEANS OF GRACE.

| | | |
|---|---|---|
| I. | Public Worship | 14 |
| II. | Class Meetings | 15 |
| III. | Love Feasts and Society Meetings | 15 |
| IV. | Prayer Meetings | 16 |
| V. | Open Air Preaching | 17 |
| VI. | Watch-Night and Renewal of the Covenant | 17 |
| VII. | The Sacraments | 17 |
| VIII. | Days of Fasting | 19 |
| IX. | Family Worship | 19 |

## CHAPTER IV.

# THE MINISTRY.

|      |                                         | PAGE |
|------|-----------------------------------------|------|
| I.   | Office and Duty of a Methodist Minister | 20   |
| II.  | Candidates for the Ministry             | 24   |
| III. | Candidates on the List of Reserve, &c.  | 27   |
| IV.  | Preachers on Trial                      | 28   |
| V.   | Admission into Full Connexion           | 30   |
| VI.  | Marriage of Ministers                   | 31   |
| VII. | The Itinerancy                          | 31   |
| VIII.| Duties of Superintendent Ministers      | 33   |
| IX.  | Supernumerary Ministers                 | 35   |
| X.   | Resignation of Ministers                | 35   |
| XI.  | Trial and Exclusion of Ministers        | 36   |
| XII. | Local Preachers                         | 38   |

## CHAPTER V.

# THE CONFERENCE.

|      |                                     |    |
|------|-------------------------------------|----|
| I.   | The Legal Conference                | 42 |
| II.  | The Irish Conference                | 45 |
| III. | Officers of the Conference          | 52 |
| IV.  | The Stationing Committee            | 54 |
| V.   | The General Committee of Management | 55 |
| VI.  | The Committee of Privileges         | 58 |

## CHAPTER VI.

# DISTRICT MEETINGS.

|      |                            |    |
|------|----------------------------|----|
| I.   | Origin and Design          | 59 |
| II.  | Annual District Meeting    | 59 |
| III. | Financial District Meeting | 61 |

## CONTENTS.

| | | PAGE |
|---|---|---|
| IV. | The Minor District Meeting | 61 |
| V. | Duties of Chairmen of Districts | 63 |
| VI. | Duties of Secretaries of Districts | 64 |

### CHAPTER VII.
### LOCAL OFFICERS AND MEETINGS.

| | | PAGE |
|---|---|---|
| I. | Leaders and Leaders' Meetings | 66 |
| II. | Circuit Stewards and Quarterly Meetings | 68 |
| III. | Trustees and Trustees' Meetings | 73 |
| IV. | Prayer Leaders' Meetings | 75 |
| V. | Sunday Schools—Teachers, and Committees | 76 |
| VI. | Associations, &c. | 77 |

# PART II.
# FUNDS AND INSTITUTIONS.

### CHAPTER I.
### CIRCUIT FINANCES.

| | | PAGE |
|---|---|---|
| I. | Circuit Income | 81 |
| II. | Circuit Expenditure | 82 |
| III. | Circuit Accounts | 84 |
| IV. | Ministerial Support | 85 |
| V. | Ministers' Residences | 86 |

### CHAPTER II.
### HOME MISSION AND CONTINGENT FUND.

| | | |
|---|---|---|
| I. | Origin and Design | 88 |
| II. | Sources of Income | 89 |
| III. | General Rules of Administration | 91 |
| IV. | Rules relating to Grants towards "Ordinary Expenditure" | 93 |

## CONTENTS.

|      |                                                                              | PAGE |
|------|------------------------------------------------------------------------------|------|
| V.   | Rules relating to Grants towards "Extraordinary Expenditure"                 | 94   |
| VI.  | Rules relating to Revision of Circuits and the Appointment of Additional Ministers | 97   |
| VII. | Rules relating to the General Mission                                        | 98   |
| VIII.| Rules relating to Work in the Army and Royal Navy                            | 99   |
| IX.  | Miscellaneous Regulations                                                    | 101  |

## CHAPTER III.

### FUNDS FOR MINISTERS' CHILDREN.

| I.   | The Children's Fund            | 104 |
| II.  | The Ministers' Sons' Fund      | 106 |
| III. | The Ministers' Daughters' Fund | 109 |

## CHAPTER IV.

### SUPERNUMERARY METHODIST MINISTERS' AND MINISTERS' WIDOWS' FUND.

| I.   | Origin                  | 112 |
| II.  | Designation             | 113 |
| III. | Object                  | 113 |
| IV.  | Income                  | 113 |
| V.   | Rules of Administration | 114 |

## CHAPTER V.

### THE CHAPEL FUND AND TRUST AFFAIRS.

| I.  | Origin of the Fund | 118 |
| II. | General Rules      | 119 |

|     |                                                        | PAGE |
|-----|--------------------------------------------------------|------|
| III. | Rules relating to Grants and Loans                    | 120  |
| IV. | Erections, Enlargements, Purchase, &c.                 | 122  |
| V. | Investigation by District Committee                     | 124  |
| VI. | Deeds                                                  | 124  |
| VII. | Management of Trust Property                          | 126  |
| VIII. | Insurance of Chapels                                 | 126  |
| IX. | Legal Proceedings                                      | 127  |
| X. | Sales                                                   | 127  |
| XI. | District Chapel Secretaries and Sub-Committees        | 127  |

## CHAPTER VI.

## THE HIBERNIAN AUXILIARY TO THE WESLEYAN METHODIST MISSIONARY SOCIETY.

|     |                                                                                   |      |
|-----|-----------------------------------------------------------------------------------|------|
| I. | Origin                                                                             | 130  |
| II. | Regulations concerning the Collection and Transmission of Funds                  | 130  |
| III. | Regulations concerning the Grant from the Parent Committee for Missionary purposes in Ireland | 131 |
| IV. | Missionary Deputations                                                            | 132  |

## CHAPTER VII.

## TRUSTEES FOR BEQUESTS.    134

## CHAPTER VIII.

## EDUCATIONAL INSTITUTIONS AND COMMITTEES.

|     |                                             |      |
|-----|---------------------------------------------|------|
| I. | Sunday Schools                               | 136  |
| II. | General Education—Primary Daily Schools    | 137  |
| III. | Wesley College, Dublin                    | 143  |
| IV. | Methodist College, Belfast                 | 145  |

## CHAPTER IX.

## THE METHODIST ORPHAN SOCIETY AND FEMALE ORPHAN SCHOOL.

|      |                                   | PAGE |
|------|-----------------------------------|------|
| I.   | The Methodist Orphan Society      | 157  |
| II.  | The Methodist Female Orphan School | 159  |

## CHAPTER X.

## TEMPERANCE COMMITTEE    163

### APPENDICES.

| | | |
|---|---|---|
| I. | Mr. Wesley's Deed of Declaration, or Deed Poll | 169 |
| II. | Digest of the Marriage Laws, so far as they affect the Ministers and Members of the Methodist Church in Ireland | 179 |
| III. | The Law relating to Burials | 192 |

INDEX .. .. .. .. .. .. .. 197

# PART I.

## CONSTITUTION AND GOVERNMENT.

# PART I.

## CONSTITUTION AND GOVERNMENT.

### CHAPTER I.

### ORIGIN OF METHODISM.

1 The origin of Methodism in England is clearly and succinctly described by the Rev. John Wesley in the introduction to the General Rules of the Methodist Societies. It arose not according to any preconceived plan, but as the result of an extensive revival of experimental and practical religion. This revival produced in the minds of those who were the subjects of it, a deep conviction of "the individual obligation and attainableness of inward and outward holiness;" and led to "intense earnestness" for the personal realization of this experience. Earnestness in the pursuit of holiness led to association for their common purpose on the part of those who were of one mind in this matter; and thus came into operation "that habit of fellowship, that systematic mutual edification," by means of the Class Meeting, "which forms so striking a feature of correspondence between Methodism and the primitive Church." The Class Meeting was the germ of the Methodist Societies; it became an arrangement and appliance not only for mutual edification, but also for securing effective oversight of each individual member; and in it the

system of Methodist finance had its origin. As Class Meetings multiplied, Leaders, Leaders' Meetings, and Stewards became necessary; and they arose as needed. As the great religious awakening spread, the system of itinerant and lay preaching sprang up as a necessity "for the continuance of the work which God had begun;" and this led to the adoption, from time to time, of suitable regulations to guide the workers. Thus Methodism has gradually assumed its present organization under the providential hand of God; new agencies being created, and new rules for guidance and government being adopted as the new and growing demands of the Church seemed to require them.

2  Methodism was introduced into Ireland in 1747, and speedily took root in many parts of the country. There are few places where it has won more glorious triumphs than in this land; and that, notwithstanding most formidable difficulties. Throughout the entire period of its history hundreds of its members, from year to year, have found a home in other lands, so that no section of the Methodist family is more widespread and influential.

3  The fundamental Rules of the Methodist Society are those published by the Rev. John Wesley in the year 1743, under the title, "The Nature, Design, and General Rules of the United Societies in London, Bristol, and Newcastle-upon-Tyne."

They are as follows:—

## GENERAL RULES

#### OF THE SOCIETY OF THE PEOPLE CALLED METHODISTS.

1. IN the latter end of the year 1739 eight or ten persons came to me in London, who appeared to be deeply convinced of sin, and earnestly groaning for redemption. They desired (as did two or three more the next day) that I would spend

some time with them in prayer, and advise them how to flee from the wrath to come, which they saw continually hanging over their heads. That we might have more time for this great work, I appointed a day when they might all come together; which, from thenceforward, they did every week, viz., on Thursday in the evening. To these, and as many more as desired to join with them, (for their number increased daily,) I gave those advices from time to time which I judged most needful for them; and we always concluded our meetings with prayer suitable to their several necessities.

2. This was the rise of the UNITED SOCIETY, first in *London*, and then in other places. Such a Society is no other than " *a company of men having the form, and seeking the power, of Godliness; united in order to pray together, to receive the word of exhortation, and to watch over one another in love, that they may help each other to work out their salvation.*"

3. That it may the more easily be discerned whether they are indeed working out their own salvation, each Society is divided into smaller companies, called Classes, according to their respective places of abode. There are about twelve persons in every Class; one of whom is styled *the Leader*. It is his business,

(1.) To see each person in his Class once a week, at least, in order

To inquire how their souls prosper;

To advise, reprove, comfort, or exhort, as occasion may require;

To receive what they are willing to give towards the support of the Gospel:

(2.) To meet the Ministers and the Stewards of the Society once a week, in order

To inform the Minister of any that are sick, or of any that walk disorderly, and will not be reproved.

To pay to the Stewards what they have received of their several Classes in the week preceding; and

To show their account of what each person has contributed.

4. There is one only condition previously required of those who desire admission into these Societies; viz., *"a desire to flee from the wrath to come, and be saved from their sins."* But wherever this is really fixed in the soul, it will be shown by its fruits. It is therefore expected of all who continue therein, that they should continue to evidence their desire of salvation,

*First,* By doing no harm; by avoiding evil in every kind, especially that which is most generally practised. Such as

The taking the name of God in vain:

The profaning the day of the Lord, either by doing ordinary work thereon, or by buying or selling:

Drunkenness; *buying* or *selling spirituous liquors;* or *drinking them,* unless in cases of extreme necessity.

*Fighting, quarrelling, brawling,* brother *going to law* with brother; returning *evil for evil,* or *railing for railing;* the *using many words* in buying or selling:

The *buying* or *selling uncustomed goods:*

The *giving* or *taking things on usury,* viz., unlawful interest:

*Uncharitable* or *unprofitable* conversation; particularly speaking evil of Magistrates, or of Ministers.

Doing to others as we would not they should do unto us:

Doing what we know is not for the glory of God; as,

The *putting on of gold and costly apparel;*

The *taking such diversions* as cannot be used in the name of the Lord Jesus.

The *singing* those *songs,* or *reading* those *books,* which do not tend to the knowledge or love of God:

Softness, and needless self-indulgence:

Laying up treasure upon earth:

Borrowing without a probability of paying; or taking up goods without a probability of paying for them.

5. It is expected of all who continue in these Societies, that they should continue to evidence their desire of salvation,

*Secondly,* By doing good, by being in every kind merciful after their power, as they have opportunity; doing good of every possible sort, and as far as is possible to all men:

To their bodies, of the ability that God giveth, by giving food to the hungry, by clothing the naked, by visiting or helping them that are sick or in prison:

To their souls, by instructing, *reproving,* or exhorting all they have any intercourse with; trampling under foot that enthusiastic doctrine of devils, that "we are not to do good, unless *our hearts be free to it.*"

By doing good, especially to them that are of the household of faith, or groaning so to be; employing them preferably to others, buying one of another, helping each other in business; and so much the more, because the world will love its own, and them *only.*

By all possible *diligence* and *frugality,* that the Gospel be not blamed.

By running with patience the race that is set before them, *denying themselves, and taking up their cross daily;* submitting to bear the reproach of Christ; to be as the filth and offscouring of the world; and looking that men should *say all manner of evil of them falsely, for the Lord's sake.*

6. It is expected of all who desire to continue in these Societies, that they should continue to evidence their desire of salvation,

*Thirdly,* By attending upon all the ordinances of God: such are

The public worship of God;

The ministry of the Word, either read or expounded;
The Supper of the Lord;
Family and private prayer;
Searching the Scriptures; and
Fasting or abstinence.

7. These are the General Rules of our Societies; all which we are taught of God to observe, even in his written Word,—the only rule, and the sufficient rule, both of our faith and practice. And all these we know his Spirit writes on every truly awakened heart. If there be any among us who observe them not, who habitually break any of them, let it be made known unto them who watch over that soul, as they that must give an account. We will admonish him of the error of his ways: we will bear with him for a season. But then, if he repent not, he hath no more place among us. We have delivered our own souls.

*May* 1, 1743.

JOHN WESLEY
CHARLES WESLEY.

## CHAPTER II.

## MEMBERS.

### I. ADMISSION OF MEMBERS.

**4** In order to prevent improper persons insinuating themselves into the Society:—

1. Let no persons be given tickets of membership till they have been at least two months on trial, and have been recommended by the Leader in whose Class they have met.

2. Let no persons be given notes of admission on trial unless recommended by one known to the Minister, or till they have met three or four times in Class.

3. Let the Rules of the Society be given to them the first time they meet.

4. If there be in the opinion of a Leader any reasonable objection to the character and conduct of any person who is on trial, such objection may be stated at the Leaders' Meeting; and if the validity of the objection be established to the satisfaction of the Meeting, a ticket of membership shall not be given to the person so objected against at that quarterly visitation.

### II. REMOVAL OF MEMBERS.

**5** When any Members of the Society remove from one Circuit to another, a certificate shall in each case be furnished by one of the Ministers to the person removing, sealed and directed to the Superintendent of the Circuit to which the Member is about to remove. At the same time a note shall be sent to the Superintendent by post informing him of the intended removal.

6 Each Superintendent shall be required to keep a list of the names of Members of Society leaving his Circuit, with an account of the places to which they remove, together with the date of the letter sent by post as above directed. The Conference recommends the use of the Book of Removals, published at the Book Room in London, for this purpose.

7 Each Superintendent shall also keep in a proper book a list of all Members received from other Circuits with an account of the places from which they came; and shall, within a reasonable time after receiving notice of removal, write to the Superintendent by whom the notice was sent, acknowledging its receipt.

8 In the March quarter a complete list of such removals and receptions for the year then ending shall be sent by each Superintendent to the Chairman of his District, not later than the last day of the month; and on receiving such lists the Chairman shall carefully examine them, and shall prepare a list of the names of persons who have removed to, or have been received from other Districts, and shall forward such lists to the respective Chairmen in sufficient time before the May District Meeting. Every Chairman is required to ascertain, by inquiry at the District Meeting, whether the persons so reported have been duly received and entered upon the roll of Members in the Circuits to which they have removed.

N.B.—Members removing to any place out of Ireland are to be set down as Emigrants.

### III. ON CONFORMITY TO THE WORLD.

9 Dancing is regarded as one of the fashions of the world which must not be permitted to gain ground among the

Members of Society; and it is directed that any of them who keep boarding schools are not to admit of, or in any respect employ dancing masters for the young people entrusted to their care.

10  While the New Testament gives no specific directions in regard to dress, yet its spirit is manifestly against the use of costly or gaudy apparel, and the wearing of needless ornaments; therefore let Ministers discourage in the Society whatever in this respect is contrary to Christian simplicity; and, in order to do this, let them read the "Thoughts upon Dress" at least once a year, in every Society where such counsels seem to be needed.

11  In the judgment of the Conference it is wrong to buy or sell lottery tickets, or to engage in raffling; and Superintendents are directed to exclude any Member of Society who may continue the practice.

12  It is also recommended to all the Members of the Societies to avoid all needless self-indulgence, and especially the use of tobacco in every form; a custom injurious both to their health and their circumstances, and unbecoming them as professed followers of Jesus Christ.

### IV. BANKRUPTCY OF MEMBERS.

13  If any Member of Society fails in business, compounds with his creditors, or becomes bankrupt, he shall be required to present to such persons as may be deputed by the Leaders' Meeting for the purpose, a full statement of his affairs; and if it be found that he has not kept fair accounts, or has been concerned in the practice of giving accommodation bills, let him be placed on his trial before a Leaders' Meeting.

14  If any Member be found to have speculated in business beyond a reasonable probability of his being able to meet every lawful demand, let him be suspended from the privileges of the Society for one year at least.

**15** If any Member who has formerly failed in business shall afterwards, by the blessing of God, have acquired property, it is expected that he will demonstrate his integrity by paying all his former deficiencies as soon as possible.

### V. MARRIAGE OF MEMBERS.

**16** Members of Society sometimes have married with ungodly persons. This has had bad effects; they have either had a cross for life, or have turned back to the world. To discourage this let the Ministers enforce the Apostle's caution "Be ye not unequally yoked together with unbelievers" (2 Cor. vi. 14); and let them exhort all to take no step in so weighty a matter without earnest prayer to God and consultation with judicious Christian friends.

**17** In general, no young woman should marry without the consent, much less without the knowledge, of her parents or guardians. Nevertheless there may be exceptional cases, as when they refuse to allow her to marry at all, or when they refuse to allow her to marry any Christian; but even in such cases she should seriously consult with those competent to give godly counsel.

**18** When the marriage is solemnized in a Methodist Chapel, or by Special Licence issued by the Secretary of the Conference, the celebrant must be a Minister in Full Connexion with the Conference.

**19** The form for the Celebration of Matrimony should be that set forth in the Book of Offices published by the Book Room in London.

### VI. OBSERVANCE OF THE LORD'S DAY.

**20** The religious observance of the Christian Sabbath, or the Lord's Day, is strictly enjoined upon all Members of the Methodist Societies. Buying or selling upon that day is prohibited, except in the case of medicine for the sick, or of supplying necessaries for funerals; and it is not considered lawful to send, deliver, or carry home work or goods.

21 The Conference directs its Ministers to exhort the Societies to make the best and most religious use of the rest and leisure of the Lord's Day; and to admonish any persons who shall be found to neglect public worship under pretence of visiting the sick or other similar engagements.

22 The Conference also directs its Ministers to show to their people the evil of *wasting* those portions of the Sabbath which are not spent in public worship, in visits or in receiving company, to the neglect of private prayer, of the perusal of the Scriptures, and of family duties, and often to the serious spiritual injury of servants, who are thus improperly employed and deprived of the public means of grace; and Ministers are required to set an example in this matter, by refusing for themselves and for their families to spend in visits, when there is no call of duty or necessity, the sacred hours of the holy Sabbath.

23 Ministers are directed not to allow the Lord's Day to be *secularized* by meetings of mere *business*, when such business refers only to the *temporal affairs* of the Church of God.

### VII. SUPPORT OF THE MINISTRY.

24 The duty of Christians to contribute according to their ability, to the support of their Ministers, rests upon the most obvious principles of justice, and is clearly recognised and enforced in the New Testament.

25 In the Methodist Societies the original rule was, that every Member should contribute "one penny weekly (unless he is in extreme poverty) and one shilling quarterly;" and every Superintendent Minister was directed to explain to the Societies the reasonableness of this rule. These subscriptions

were paid at the regular weekly and quarterly Meeting of the Classes.

**26** But, even in the beginning, this Rule was not intended to measure and limit the contributions of the Members of the Societies for the support of the Ministry, and the carrying on of the "work of God." It was expected that every man's "beneficence" should "increase in the same proportion as his substance, if he would shun the guilt and the curse of covetousness."

**27** In Irish Methodism it very early became the usage to take up a collection in every regular Congregation at the public Services on the Lord's Day; thus giving to all who attended on the ministry of the Word the opportunity of bearing their part in supporting the ordinances of the Gospel established and maintained for their benefit. This connection of *contribution* with *Worship*, the Conference judges to be eminently Scriptural; and it urges upon all its Congregations increased attention to the privilege and duty therein implied.

**28** Other occasions and modes of contribution for the Sustentation and Extension of the work of the Methodist Church have, from time to time, received the formal, or implied, sanction of the Conference; and, while imperative Rules have not been adopted with reference to them, they are judged to be in harmony with the spirit of the Original Rule of the Methodist Societies, and to afford suitable opportunities for the exercise of that "proportionate" and "systematic" Christian beneficence which is the bounden duty of all who will be obedient to the Gospel of Christ.

### VIII. TRIAL AND EXCLUSION OF MEMBERS.

**29** No member shall be excluded from the Society without the concurrence of a Leaders' Meeting, where such Meeting can be obtained; the accused member shall receive a copy of the charges made against him, together with the name of the accuser before the day appointed for the investigation.

30  If a member who is excluded from Society where no Leaders' Meeting can be had, shall feel himself aggrieved, he may appeal to the next Quarterly Meeting.

31  It is desirable that no sentence of *expulsion* shall be pronounced till a week, at least, after the trial.

32  In all cases of dissatisfaction with the sentence, or with the verdict, the aggrieved person shall have the right of appeal to the Annual District Meeting; and, if still dissatisfied, to the Conference. If it be found more convenient, the appeal in the first instance may be to a Minor District Meeting.

33  In the trial of accused Members it must ever be borne in mind that the *Law of God contained in the Holy Scriptures* is to be regarded as furnishing that *primary* standard of judgment by which the innocence or culpability of any particular acts adduced in evidence is to be determined.

34  No person who has been expelled from the Society shall be re-admitted by a succeeding Superintendent, until after consultation (if practicable) with the Superintendent who was in office at the time of the expulsion.

## CHAPTER III.

## THE MEANS OF GRACE.

### I. PUBLIC WORSHIP.

**35** The following is recognised as the usual order of Public Worship among us on the Lord's Day:—

1. The morning service consists of singing, prayer, singing, reading a lesson out of the Old Testament and a lesson out of the New Testament, singing, preaching, singing, prayer, and the benediction.

2. The same order is observed in the evening service, except that one lesson may suffice.

3. The Lord's Prayer is used on all occasions of public worship in concluding the first prayer, and the Apostolic benediction in dismissing the Congregation.

4. In administering the Ordinances, the Form contained in the Book of Offices is used.

5. The people should, from time to time, be earnestly exhorted to take part in the public worship of God—first in singing, secondly in prayer, in the Scriptural attitude of kneeling.

6. The Conference directs the use of Wesley's Hymn Book, and strongly recommends the reading of the Hymns by the Minister conducting the Service.

7. To guard against formality in singing in public worship, (1) let the Ministers choose such hymns as are proper for the occasion, and let not too much be sung at once, seldom more than five or six verses. (2) Let the tune be suited to the words,

and let not the singing be too slow. (3) Let some suitable person be appointed to conduct the singing.

## II. CLASS MEETINGS.

**36** The origin of the Class Meeting, which is the established form of Christian fellowship among Methodists, is stated in the General Rules. (See pp. 2, 3) The Conference has resolved that, "Considering the important place which the Class Meeting holds in the history of Methodism, and its great value as an edifying means of grace, we desire to express our deep conviction that this Institution should be maintained in unimpaired influence, and, if possible, rendered more generally useful."

**37** In order to render our Class Meetings interesting and profitable, let each Leader be careful to enquire how every soul in his Class prospers; not only how he observes the outward rules, but how he grows in the knowledge and love of God; and let each Leader converse with the Minister frequently and freely.

**38** Let improper Leaders be changed. Let the Ministers see that all the Leaders are not only men of sound judgment, but men truly devoted to God.

**39** Whenever it shall appear practicable, let some active, zealous men, whose piety and general character shall be approved by the Leaders' Meeting, be employed to attempt the formation of new Classes in suitable neighbourhoods.

**40** Let the Ministers affectionately, but firmly, enforce on the Leaders, as an essential part of our pastoral discipline, the Rule of the Society which states it to be the duty of a Leader "to see each person in his Class once a week, at least."

## III. LOVE FEASTS AND SOCIETY MEETINGS.

**41** A Love Feast shall be held in each Circuit and

Mission Station once a quarter; admission to which should be by the ticket of membership, or by a note from the Minister.

2. The money collected at the Love Feast should be given to the poor.

3. No Love Feast shall be held without the approbation of the Superintendent of the Circuit.

**42** A Society Meeting shall be held once a quarter, whenever it is practicable, by the Superintendent, or by his colleague acting under his directions.

The principal object of the Meeting shall be the spiritual edification of the Church, by exhortation on the part of the Minister present, with prayer and other religious exercises. The members shall be faithfully admonished respecting their religious and Christian deportment, their closet and family duties, and their attendance upon the public and private means of grace.

**43** Superintendents are directed to appoint a Special Society Meeting to be held in the principal Chapel in their Circuits, either on the Lord's Day, or on some convenient evening of the week for the purpose of having the Pastoral Address read to the Society, and made the subject of suitable remarks and exhortations.

### IV. PRAYER MEETINGS.

**44** Prayer Meetings should be held not only in the Chapels, but also in private houses, or other suitable places, in different parts of a town or neighbourhood, at such times as do not interfere with our general worship.

**45** Missionary Prayer Meetings should be held monthly, when convenient, in the principal Chapels, at which extracts from the Missionary Notices should be read, information on the subject of Christian Missions given, and united supplication for the salvation of the world offered up.

**46** In country places where a full supply of preaching cannot be arranged for, let suitable persons belonging to the nearest Society be appointed by the Superintendent Minister to attend and conduct services of prayer and exhortation, or to read a sermon to the Congregation.

### V. OPEN AIR PREACHING.

**47** In order to promote an increase in the Congregations, and to reach many who might not otherwise hear the Gospel, let the old Methodist custom be continued of preaching out-of-doors, in the streets, or in the fields, as far as may conveniently and prudently be done.

### VI. WATCH-NIGHT AND RENEWAL OF THE COVENANT.

**48** It is an established custom to hold a religious service on the last night of the year; and also to hold one on the first Sabbath evening of the new year, for the purpose of, what is termed, the *Renewal of our Covenant with God*.

### VII. THE SACRAMENTS.

#### (1.) *Baptism*.

**49** The Sacrament of Baptism shall, if possible, be always administered in the public Congregation, and, in general, only to the children of our own members and those of our regular hearers. The Form provided in the Book of Offices shall be used in the administration.

**50** No Preacher on Trial shall administer this Sacrament, except with the express sanction of the Superintendent; and this sanction shall extend only to private administration in cases where there are circumstances of great emergency which will not allow the administration to be conveniently delayed.

**51** All Baptisms shall forthwith be registered by the Officiating Minister in the Baptismal Register of the Circuit.

**52** With regard to Certificates of Baptism, copied from the Register, the Law requires that a penny stamp be affixed to each Certificate, and authorizes that a fee of one shilling be claimed by the Minister furnishing the Certificate.

**53** Registers of Baptisms previous to 1837 are, for the most part, in the General Register in the Conference Safe in Dublin; and Certificates may be obtained from the Superintendent Minister of the Stephen's Green Circuit.

### (2.) *The Lord's Supper.*

**54** The Lord's Supper shall be administered in all the principal Chapels of the town Societies once a month, and in the country Chapels at least once a quarter.

**55** The administration shall be by the Superintendent, or other Minister being in Full Connexion; the Form used in the administration shall be that provided in the Connexional Book of Offices.

**56** Admission to the Lord's Supper shall be granted to all members of the Society, and to such of the regular members of the Congregation as may be judged eligible by the Minister.

**57** In order to obviate, as far as possible, all cause of conscientious objection on the part of any to unite in the Communion of the Lord's Supper, it is strongly recommended that *the purest natural wine* which can be conveniently procured shall be used in all Congregations in the celebration of this sacred ordinance.

**58** Should there be in any Societies those who allege conscientious objections, and who may request on their own behalf, that the *fruit of the vine* in some other form shall be used in this ordinance, the Superintendent of the Circuit, taking council with the Chairman of the District, *may make provision* for these special and exceptional cases; provided always that *nothing which is not the fruit of the vine* shall be used in the ordinance, and that no mode of administration shall be adopted which has a tendency to divide our members into two classes, or be inconsistent with the foregoing resolutions.

### VIII. DAYS OF FASTING.

59 As the best human arrangements for the promotion of the work of God among men can be of no avail unless succeeded by the Divine blessing, the Conference has appointed the first Friday in September, December, March, and June, to be observed as days of fasting, humiliation, and prayer, for the special outpouring of the Holy Spirit upon all our Ministers, Societies, and Congregations, and upon the community at large, in order to the removal of the hindrances to the spread of the Gospel in the land, and the revival of that religion which is pure and undefiled.

### IX. FAMILY WORSHIP.

60 Let not family worship be neglected, or observed in a dull and formal manner; therefore let the Ministers strongly recommend, both in public and private, the having family prayer, morning and evening, after reading a portion of Scripture; and let no head of a family who neglects this important duty continue in the Society.

61 Though extemporary prayer in families is greatly to be preferred, yet if no one in the family has the gift of extemporary prayer let suitable forms of prayer be used; and, wherever it is practicable, let all heads of families see that all members of the family, both children and servants, are present at family worship.

# CHAPTER IV.

# THE MINISTRY.

### I. OFFICE AND DUTY OF A METHODIST MINISTER.

**62** The design of God in raising up the Methodist Ministry may reasonably be believed to have been to assist in spreading Scriptural holiness over the land.

**63** The office of a Christian Minister is to watch over souls, as he that must give account; and in order to do this he must feed and guide the flock.

**64** The duty of a Methodist Minister, in addition to regular and faithful preaching, is to meet the Societies and Classes, to meet the Leaders, to visit the people of his charge, especially the sick, and to attend to all parts of the Methodist discipline.

**65** The following are the Rules of conduct originally published by Mr Wesley under the title—

#### RULES OF A HELPER.

1. Be diligent. Never be unemployed a moment. Never be triflingly employed. Never while away time: neither spend any more time at any place than is strictly necessary.

2. Be serious. Let your motto be, "Holiness to the Lord." Avoid all lightness, jesting, and foolish talking.

3. Converse sparingly and cautiously with women, particularly with young women.

4. Take no step towards marriage, without first consulting with your brethren.

5. Believe evil of no one; unless you see it done, take heed how you credit it. Put the best construction on every thing. You know the judge is always supposed to be on the prisoner's side.

6. Speak evil of no one; else *your* word *especially* would eat as doth a canker. Keep your thoughts within your own breast, till you come to the person concerned.

7. Tell every one what you think wrong in him, and that plainly, as soon as may be, else it will fester in your heart; make all haste to cast the fire out of your bosom.

8. Do not affect the gentleman. You have no more to do with this character than with that of a dancing master. A preacher of the Gospel is the servant of all.

9. Be ashamed of nothing but sin; not of fetching wood (if time permit) or drawing water, nor of cleaning your own shoes, or your neighbour's.

10. Be punctual. Do everything exactly at the time. And, in general, do not mend our rules, but keep them, not for wrath, but for conscience sake.

11. You have nothing to do but to save souls. Therefore spend and be spent in this work. And go always, not only to those that want you, but to those that want you most.

Observe. It is not your business to preach so many times and to take care of this and that Society, but to save as many souls as you can; to bring as many sinners as you possibly can to repentance, and with all your power to build them up in that holiness, without which they cannot see the Lord. And remember! a Methodist preacher is to mind every point, great and small, in the Methodist discipline. Therefore you will need all the sense you have, and to have all your wits about you.

12. Act in all things, not according to your own will, but as a son in the Gospel. As such it is your part to employ your time in the manner which we direct, partly in preaching and visiting from house to house; and partly in reading, meditation, and prayer. Above all, if you labour with us in the Lord's vineyard, it is needful that you should do that part of the work which we advise, at those times and places which we judge most for His glory.

66 Resolutions have been, from time to time, adopted by the Conference with reference to the "Office and Duty" of the Methodist Ministry to the following effect:—

1. Any Minister who engages in trade and will not relinquish it shall cease to be recognised as a member of the Conference.

2. Ministers should not speak disparagingly of each other, but should defend one another's character, so far as is consistent with truth; should labour in honour, each to prefer the other before himself; and should never on any Circuit take part against the Superintendent.

3. They should visit from house to house, and endeavour to get every one therein to become a Christian in all inward and outward holiness.

4. They should consider themselves the spiritual guides of the children of their people, should pay particular attention to their spiritual welfare, and should arrange for weekly meetings, either in the Sunday School or in Special Classes for the purpose, that they may receive suitable religious instruction.

5. They should endeavour in their public ministry to preach all those leading and vital doctrines of the Gospel, for the proclamation of which the early Methodist Preachers were distinguished, and to preach them in the primitive method: evangelically, experimentally, zealously, and plainly,

giving to them a decided prominence in every sermon, and labouring to apply them closely, affectionately and energetically to the conscience of their hearers.

6. They should consecrate themselves fully and entirely to their proper work, as servants of Christ and His Church, giving themselves wholly to it, both in public and in private, and guarding against all occupations of their time and thoughts which have no direct connection with their great calling, and which would injuriously divert their attention from the momentous task of saving souls, and taking care of the flock of Christ.

7. They should covet earnestly the best gifts, to qualify them for an acceptable and useful ministry; should seek them in prayer from Him who is the Father of lights and fountain of wisdom; should "stir up" and improve by study and diligent cultivation "the gift that is in them," and should strive in every way to be workmen who need not to "be ashamed, rightly dividing the word of truth."

8. They should frequently read and carefully study Wesley's "Rules of a Helper" and other directions of the Conference which relate to the duties of a Preacher and Pastor.

9. They should try to open new preaching places, try again places that may have been given up, be attentive to the supply and superintendence of places on the plan, and should not be satisfied until every town, village, and hamlet in their respective neighbourhoods are blessed, so far as they can accomplish it, with the means of grace and salvation. In a word, all Ministers should consider themselves as called to be, as to enterprise, zeal and diligence, home missionaries, and to enlarge and extend, as well as keep, the Circuits to which they are appointed.

10. They should pay particular attention to backsliders, and endeavour, in the spirit of meekness, to restore them that

have been overtaken in a fault, and by private efforts, as well as by public ministrations to recover the fallen out of the snare of the devil.

11. They should remember and endeavour to impress on their people that Methodism, as a Church, does not exist for the purposes of party; and that Methodists are especially bound by the example of their founder, by the original principles on which their Societies were formed, and by their constant professions before the world, to avoid a narrow, bigoted and sectarian spirit; to abstain from needless and unprofitable disputes; and as far as they innocently can, to please all men for their good unto edification.

12. Methodist Ministers, therefore, should maintain toward all denominations of Christians who hold the Head, the kind and Catholic spirit of Original Methodism, and according to the noble maxim of their father in the Gospel, "Be the friends of all, the enemies of none."

## II. CANDIDATES FOR THE MINISTRY.

**67** Before any person is recommended as a Candidate for the Ministry, he must be nominated by the Superintendent Minister at the Quarterly Meeting of the Circuit in which he is a member and a Local-preacher. If the Quarterly Meeting approve, he may be recommended by the Superintendent to the Annual District Meeting to be admitted to the usual examinations.

**68** No Candidate shall be accepted who does not possess a fair acquaintance with English Grammar and Orthography, Arithmetic, Geography, and English History.

**69** If any Candidate shall not have resided for two years in succession on the Circuit from which it is proposed to recommend him, the Superintendent of such Circuit shall, previous to taking any other steps, correspond on the subject with the Superintendent of the Circuit in which he has resided.

**70** All Candidates shall be examined, by papers, in the Holy Scriptures and Wesley's First Fifty-three Sermons, and shall be required to write an Essay on some given doctrine or book of Scripture. Examination papers and subject of Essay shall be supplied to Superintendents during the month of March in each year, on application to the Secretary of the Committee of Examiners, and the examination shall be conducted under the supervision of the respective Superintendents in the first week of April.

**71** Before any Candidate for the Ministry is recommended for admission on trial, he shall be heard preach by at least three Ministers of the District Committee previous to its meeting in May, including the Superintendent who recommends him; and they shall present to the District Meeting a written report, with their signatures attached, which report, should the Candidate be recommended by the Committee, shall be inserted in its Minutes.

**72** In the presence of the members of the District Meeting, the Candidate shall be required:—

1. To give a brief account of his conversion to God, what he believes to be his call to the Ministry, and his present religious experience.

2. He shall then be examined by the Chairman of the District (or by some Minister appointed by him) as to his acquaintance with the Doctrines and Institutions of Christianity; his knowledge of Mr Wesley's writings, and of the Methodist discipline. He shall also be examined as to his literary acquirements and shall be questioned as to whether he drinks drams or uses snuff or tobacco, and whether he is free from matrimonial engagement or secular encumbrances.

N.B. Any Candidate who uses snuff or tobacco shall not be recommended as a probationer.

**73** The strictest attention to the Holy Scriptures shall be urged upon every Candidate for the Ministry, as no one can be received as a probationer who is not able to show a thorough acquaintance with the Word of God.

**74** Chairmen of Districts are required not only to examine very minutely in their District Meetings all who are proposed as Candidates for the Ministry, but also to return in the District Minutes, for the consideration of the Conference, and to forward to the Special Examination Committee the opinion of the District Meetings, after such examination, of their health, piety, moral character, ministerial abilities, belief of Methodist doctrines, attachment to Methodist discipline, and freedom from debt, as well as from all other secular encumbrances. In the same District Minutes, the Minister who recommends any Candidate shall give the exact date of his birth, and also a recommendatory character, which shall be forthwith copied, if the Conference receive such Candidate upon trial, into the book provided for that purpose.

**75** All Candidates who have passed their respective District Meetings shall appear before a Special Examination Committee, to meet in Dublin in the month of May. This Committee, shall make minute inquiry into their literary attainments, the state of their health, and all other matters affecting their suitability for our work. After careful consideration of all the circumstances of each case, the Committee shall recommend the allocation of all whom they consider suitable severally—(1) for the Methodist College, (2) for Circuit Work, (3) for the List of Reserve.

**76** All Candidates shall furnish to the District Meeting, upon a form provided for the purpose, a certificate from a physician as to the state of their health. These certificates shall be forwarded by the Chairmen of Districts to the Secretary of the Special Examination Committee.

### III. CANDIDATES ON THE LIST OF RESERVE AND AT THE METHODIST COLLEGE.

**77** When there are a larger number of Candidates for the Ministry accepted by the Conference than can be appointed to Circuits or admitted to the Theological Institution in the Methodist College, their names are placed on a List of Reserve to be placed in the hands of the Vice-President for the time being.

**78** All applications for Supplies for Circuits from the List of Reserve, rendered necessary by the continued illness, or death, or resignation, or suspension of Ministers, must be made to the Vice-President of the Conference through the Chairman of the District in which the Supply is needed.

**79** Provision cannot be made for sending a temporary Supply from the List of Reserve, inasmuch as this involves the calling out of an additional Minister. All arrangements for temporary supplies must be made within the District in which the vacancies occur, and with the sanction of the Chairman of the District.

**80** Any Candidate on the List of Reserve appointed by the Vice-President to a Circuit before November 1st, shall be regarded as entering on the first year of probation, and shall be treated accordingly at the Annual District Meeting.

**81** It is most desirable that all Candidates sent to the Methodist College shall possess a fair acquaintance with the elements of Latin and Greek.

**82** Each Candidate for the Ministry who is sent to the Methodist College shall be required, on entering, to pledge himself to pay to the Governors of the College compensation for his board, residence, and training, in the event of his retiring from the work before he has rendered ten years of active service. For this purpose the estimated cost in each case shall be £60 per annum.

83  Should the Candidate be under twenty-one years of age at the time of entrance, his parent or guardian, or some other accepted security, shall be required to sign a guarantee to the same effect.

84  Accepted Candidates who are appointed to Circuits shall have permission during their probation to express through their respective District Meetings, a desire for admission to the Methodist College; and if the Conference grant such request, the time which they have travelled shall be regarded as a part of their probation.

85  In the case of young men who may claim to have travelled a year, whether by the appointment of the Conference or from the List of Reserve, and who may have subsequently been sent to the College or transferred from the College to the List of Reserve without an appointment, the time during which they may so continue at the College or on the List of Reserve without a regular appointment to Circuit work, shall not be counted in their years of travelling.

86  As a rule, two years shall be the period of a Candidate's residence in the College; special cases of shorter or longer stay are left to the judgment of the College officials, to whose direction the Conference also commits the course of study for Candidates.

#### IV. PREACHERS ON TRIAL.

87  Each Candidate accepted by the Conference shall continue on trial for a period of four years; except when by special resolution of the Conference a shorter period is stated to be sufficient.

88  A Course of Study prescribed by the Conference for each year during which probationers continue on trial shall be carefully gone through by them.

89  A Committee appointed by the Conference shall draw up a series of Examination Papers on above course of study,

and Forms of Report, which shall be printed under the direction of the Secretary of the Committee, and by him, during the month of March in each year, supplied to the Superintendents who have Preachers on Trial under their charge, in sufficient time for the examinations in April.

90 It shall be required of all Preachers on Trial who have been students at the Methodist College, that they shall take the prescribed course in Greek. Other probationers, who do not take the prescribed course in Greek, shall be required to take the corresponding portions of Scripture in English.

91 The written examinations of Preachers on Trial, and of Candidates, shall be conducted under the supervision of their respective Superintendents in the first week of April. The papers, both printed and written, shall be forwarded without delay to the Secretary of the Examination Committee, who shall send them to the Examiners for their Reports, and shall transmit the results to the respective Chairmen of Districts, in time for the May District Meetings.

92 Each Superintendent shall exercise, either personally or by a competent representative, a constant supervision of the young brethren while engaged on the Examination Papers, taking care that no use shall be permitted of book or manuscript of any kind whatsoever.

93 The Secretary of the Examination Committee shall, in each year, direct the special attention of the Conference to the case of those Preachers on Trial who do not obtain a general average in their marks of forty-five per cent.

94 Every Preacher on Trial is required to deliver to the Chairman of his District a list of the books which he has read during the year. These lists shall be laid before the Meeting, that the senior brethren may have the opportunity of giving the junior preachers such advice and directions concerning their studies as may appear to be necessary.

**95** Every Preacher on Trial shall be required to preach a sermon each year at the District Meeting, during the period of his probation; and the judgment of the District Meeting respecting such sermons shall be recorded in the Minutes.

**96** Any Preacher who marries, while on trial, without the express permission of the Conference, thereby ceases to be recognised as a Methodist preacher.

## V. ADMISSION INTO FULL CONNEXION.

**97** "The Conference shall, and may, admit into Connexion with them any person or persons whom they shall approve to be preachers and expounders of God's Holy Word, under the care and direction of the Conference; the name of every such person or persons, so admitted into Connexion as aforesaid, being entered in the Journals or Minutes of the Conference." (Deed of Declaration, Clause 9.)

**98** Before any Preacher on Trial is recommended by his District Committee for admission into Full Connexion, he shall undergo a careful examination by the Chairman in the Meeting, respecting his acquaintance with Wesley's works in general, especially with his Sermons and his Notes on the New Testament, in addition to the other examinations required by existing rules; and no Preacher on Trial shall be so recommended unless the result of the examination be satisfactory to the Meeting.

**99** A theological examination of Candidates for admission into Full Connexion shall take place at the Conference at a time when the President can attend, and when a large proportion of the Conference, including its official members, may be expected to be present.

**100** If the result of these examinations be satisfactory to the Conference, and the Candidates are received into Full Connexion, they shall be set apart to the work of the ministry, by the imposition of hands, and by giving to each of them a copy of the Holy Scriptures, and also a copy of the Larger Minutes inscribed thus: "As long as you freely consent to, and earnestly endeavour to walk by these Rules, we shall rejoice to acknowledge you as a fellow-labourer."

### VI. MARRIAGE OF MINISTERS.

**101** Ministers who contemplate marriage are strongly advised not to take any step in the matter without first consulting with their ministerial brethren.

**102** No Minister shall contract marriage with any woman who has a parent or parents living, until he shall have unequivocally the consent of such parent or parents; and if he do marry without such consent, he shall be either suspended or expelled, according to the circumstances of the case.

**103** If any Minister marry a woman who is under age and has no parents alive, without the consent of her guardian or guardians, he shall be subject to discipline as above.

**104** When any Minister has married, the ensuing May District Meeting is directed carefully to inquire whether he has complied with the apostolical injunction, binding on all Christians, but more especially on all Christian Ministers, to marry only "in the Lord"; and if there be reason to believe the contrary, the Chairman is to report the same to the Conference.

### VII. THE ITINERANCY.

**105** The rule which regulates and provides for the Itinerancy among the Ministers and Preachers on Trial of the Conference is contained in the *Eleventh* Clause of Mr. Wesley's Deed Poll, which declares that the Conference "shall not, nor may appoint for more than three years successively, any member of the Conference, or any one admitted into Connexion with the same, or upon trial, to the use and enjoyment of any

Chapel or premises given or to be given or conveyed on the trusts" recited in the said Deed.

**106** The Conference has agreed that it shall be recognised as a general rule, that no Minister or Preacher on Trial shall be appointed for a third year to a Circuit unless a request for such appointment be presented from the Quarterly Meeting of the Circuit signed by the Circuit Stewards.

**107** The Conference has also agreed that no Minister or Preacher on Trial shall be appointed to a Circuit on which he was previously stationed unless he has been absent from it at least six years.

**108** All petitions from Circuits for the appointment of any particular Minister or Preacher on Trial, must be agreed to at a Quarterly Meeting of the Circuit, and signed by the Circuit Stewards on behalf of the Meeting.

**109** Ministers or Preachers on Trial are forbidden to use any means, directly or indirectly, to secure petitions for their own appointment.

**110** With reference to all appointments to Chaplaincies and Connexional Offices affecting Stations where the provisions of the Deed Poll do not necessitate the removal of the Minister at the end of three years, the appointment shall be from year to year for a term not exceeding six years; and it shall not be renewed unless sufficient reason be shown.

**111** The *Official* relation between a Minister and his Circuit terminates with the confirmation of the Stations by which he is appointed to another Circuit.

**112** Ministers appointed to Circuits are expected to be in their new appointments not later than the third Sunday after the close of the Conference; the particular date to be arranged by correspondence between the Ministers concerned.

## VIII. DUTIES OF SUPERINTENDENT MINISTERS.

113 In the time of Mr Wesley the Preacher appointed in charge of a Circuit was called the "Assistant"; since then the name has been changed to Superintendent. When there is more than one Minister appointed to a Circuit he whose name stands first on the list of stations is the Superintendent, who is accountable for the proper maintenance of discipline in the Circuit; his colleagues are his co-Pastors with whom he should confer on all matters affecting the interests of the Circuit, but the ultimate responsibility for action rests upon him.

Subject to the Rules and usage in regard to the different matters, it is the duty of the Superintendent—

1. To consider the Preachers on Trial as his pupils, whom he should instruct in the various details of their work, and into whose behaviour and studies he should frequently inquire; and, at proper times, into their Christian life and experience.

2. To admit into and exclude members from the Society; to arrange for the quarterly visitation of the Classes by himself or his colleagues; to keep lists of members received from or removed to other Circuits; to forward such lists to the Chairman of the District as directed (see par. 6, 7, 8); to enter all necessary particulars in the Circuit Schedule Book; to forward in due time to the proper officers of the District, all such statistical information relating to his Circuit as may be required by rule, and to send the Circuit Schedule Book, when filled up, to the Conference Safe.

3. To arrange for the holding of Society Meetings, Love Feasts, Watch-Nights, Prayer Meetings, Leaders' Meetings, and Quarterly Meetings; and to see that the Prayer Leaders' and Local Preachers' plans are duly made and fulfilled.

4. To see that the accounts of the Circuit and the Society Stewards and of the Trustees (if they have a separate account) and all other accounts pertaining to any department of Circuit work, are properly kept and duly audited.

5. To obtain the requisite sanction before proceeding with the erection, enlargement, purchase, or sale of any Trust property; to take care that all Trust property acquired in his Circuit is duly settled according to rule; that Trust Deeds are renewed as often as required; that the property is kept in good repair and used only for the purposes specified in the several Deeds.

6. To see that no stranger shall be suffered to preach in any of our places of worship unless he comes fully accredited; if an Itinerant Preacher, by having his name entered on the Minutes of the Conference of which he is a member; and if a Local Preacher, by a recommendatory note from his Superintendent.

7. To see that the Baptismal Register; the Circuit Schedule Book; the Furniture Book; the Circuit Register of Members and Classes; Lists of families belonging to the Congregation with their names and addresses; Lists of Orphans on his Circuit who are receiving grants from the Orphan Fund; with all other Books, Lists, or Forms of Return required by rule to be kept, are duly and accurately filled and kept and presented to the District Meeting, or forwarded to the Officers of Funds, or left for his successor, or otherwise dealt with as the Rules direct.

8. To see that all Collections for Connexional Funds are made at the proper time, and the amounts forthwith forwarded to the respective Treasurers.

9. To furnish lists of preaching places and members of Society to Superintendents to whose care the same may have

been transferred on account of changes which may have been authorized in Circuit boundaries.

10. To attend to all other matters and duties inherent in his office, or which may, from time to time, be specified in the Minutes of Conference.

### IX. SUPERNUMERARY MINISTERS.

**114** Supernumerary Ministers are those who on account of age, or failure in health, or other cause, which to the Conference may seem sufficient, are temporarily or permanently relieved from the duties of the full work of the ministry.

**115** Supernumerary Ministers are not at liberty to remove to England, America, or elsewhere for the purpose of settling there, without the special permission of the Conference obtained in writing; and any Supernumerary removing from Ireland to reside elsewhere without such leave shall thereby forfeit all claim on the Supernumerary Ministers' and Ministers' Widows' Fund.

**116** Any Supernumerary entering into business shall no longer be recognised as a Minister among us, and his name shall cease to appear in the published or private Minutes of the Conference. In general, Supernumerary Ministers occupying farms shall be regarded as having entered into business; but the Conference reserves to itself the right to consider each case upon its own merits.

**117** Supernumerary Ministers who may have entered into business, and who have become insolvent, shall be subject to the law which in such cases applies to all members of Society.

### X. RESIGNATION OF MINISTERS.

**118** In the case of the resignation of any Minister or Preacher on Trial, tendered to the Chairman of his District, during the interval between the sittings of Conference, the

Chairman shall consult with the Vice-President of the Conference and be governed by his direction as to ulterior measures.

119 The resignation of a Minister in Full Connexion, and of good standing, is entered in the printed Minutes of the Conference under the question "Who have ceased to be recognised as Ministers among us?"

Answer A——B——who has voluntarily retired.

If a Minister resign under charges, the answer is:—

C——D——who has retired; or, who has also retired.

120 In all cases in which credentials are applied for by Ministers or Preachers on Trial who may leave the Irish Connexion, and the Conference deems it right to grant them, such credentials shall be signed by its Secretary for the time being. The Conference disapproves of the practice of giving private testimonials, and declares that it is not accountable for any that may be so given.

XI. TRIAL AND EXCLUSION OF MINISTERS.

121 "The Conference shall and may expel and put out from being a member thereof, or from being in Connexion therewith, or from being upon Trial, any person, member of the Conference, or admitted into Connexion or upon Trial, for any cause which to the Conference may seem fit or necessary; and every member of the Conference so expelled and put out shall cease to be a member thereof, to all intents and purposes as though he was naturally dead." (Deed of Declaration, clause 8).

122 The question of ministerial character and ability engages attention at the Annual District Meeting during its pastoral session, when inquiry is made respecting every Minister and Preacher on Trial:—Is there any objection

to his moral and religious character? Does he believe and preach our doctrines? Has he duly observed and enforced our discipline? Has he competent abilities for our Itinerant work? If any member of the Meeting intends to prefer a complaint against another member he should, if there be opportunity, make known his intention to the person concerned; but the District Committee has power to institute any inquiries which may appear to be proper and requisite. In case of a charge being preferred to the Chairman of the District, previous to the Meeting, he should send to the accused an exact statement in writing of such charge, with the name of the person by whom it is preferred. The Meeting may, if it deems fit, suspend any Minister or Preacher on Trial till the Conference, to which there is in all cases the right of appeal.

123 If in the interval between the sittings of the Annual District Meetings, any charge be preferred to the Chairman of a District against any Minister or Preacher on Trial in his District, and if in the judgment of the Chairman, it be of sufficient importance to call for a prompt investigation, he shall as soon as possible submit the matter to a Minor District Meeting, and such Meeting shall have the same authority to examine into the charges alleged that the Annual District Meeting has; and shall have power, if it see fit, to suspend the accused person till the next Annual District Meeting, or till the Conference. (See Regulations concerning Minor District Meetings par. 202-208.)

124 If a Minister be expelled, his name is printed without remark in the Minutes of Conference under the question " Who have ceased to be recognised as Ministers amongst us ? "

125 The names of Preachers on Trial who may be discontinued are simply omitted in the printed Minutes.

**126** A Minister under suspension has no right to vote on any question in the Conference while his suspension is continued: nor even to be present at its meetings without leave until his own case be brought forward.

## XII. LOCAL PREACHERS.
### 1 *General Directions.*

**127** Superintendent Ministers are required to give special attention to eligible and promising young men in their respective Circuits, with a view to their becoming Local Preachers; and, as far as practicable, to assist in preparing them for this office.

**128** It is essential that persons filling the office of Local Preacher shall give due attendance upon Class-meeting, and no one neglecting this shall be appointed to or continued in the office.

**129** No one who has been suspended or expelled from the Ministry shall be employed as a Local Preacher, without the consent of the Conference previously obtained.

### 2. *Appointment and Duties.*

**130** Candidates for the office of Local Preacher shall be submitted to a term of trial of not less than one year before they are fully appointed.

**131** The nomination of persons as suitable candidates shall rest with the Superintendent Minister, and shall be made in a regular Local Preachers' Meeting, or in the Circuit Quarterly Meeting, as hereinafter provided; and no one shall be admitted on trial without the approval of the majority of such meeting.

**132** Previous to the admission of any person on trial for the office of Local Preacher, the meeting at which he is nominated shall be satisfied that he has been truly converted to God; that he gives evidence of genuine piety; that he is zealous in promoting the work of God; and that he has the ability to express himself with sufficient readiness and clearness.

133 During his term of probation, each Candidate for the office of Local Preacher shall be required, in addition to a diligent study of the Word of God, to read Mr. Wesley's fifty-three Sermons and his Notes on the New Testament.

134 Upon the termination of his year of probation, the Candidate shall be examined in the presence of the Local Preachers' Meeting, upon the following subjects:—His present religious experience; his knowledge and belief of the doctrines of Scripture as set forth in the standard works of Methodism; and his willingness to submit to Methodist discipline, and to do whatever work may be allotted to him. The Candidate shall also be required to preach a trial sermon ; and, if the result of this sermon and the examination be satisfactory to the majority of the Meeting, he shall be received, subject to the approval of the next Quarterly Meeting of the Circuit, as a fully accredited Local Preacher.

135 As a general rule, Local Preachers shall exercise their office within the bounds of their own Circuits ; but this shall not preclude them from accepting occasional appointments to preach on other Circuits, provided such are made with the knowledge and sanction of the Superintendent Ministers of those Circuits, and provided also that the work on their own Circuit is not thereby neglected.

136 In the case of a Local Preacher removing from one Circuit to another, on the production of his certificate of office, his name may be placed on the plan of the latter Circuit, with the concurrence of the Local Preachers' Meeting.

3. *Local Preachers' Meetings.*

137 In every Circuit where there are three or more Local Preachers, a Meeting shall be held not less frequently

than half-yearly, which shall consist of all the Ministers, Preachers on Trial, and Local Preachers on the Circuit. It shall annually appoint a Secretary, who shall keep a record of its proceedings, and of the attendance of its members.

138 The business of this Meeting shall be as follows:—

1. To arrange, under the direction of the Superintendent Minister, and for such a period as may be determined, a Plan of the Appointments which are to be supplied by the Local Preachers.

2. To inquire into the efficiency and faithfulness of the Local Preachers on the Plan, and to remove from the office any who are found inefficient, neglectful of appointments, or otherwise unsuitable.

N.B. This does not affect cases of discipline in which Local Preachers, as well as other members of Society, are subject to the jurisdiction of the Leaders' Meeting.

3. To judge of the suitability of persons nominated to be admitted on trial, or to be fully accredited as Local Preachers, and to receive or reject them, subject to the conditions hereinbefore mentioned.

139 At the meeting preceding the May District Meeting, a certificate shall be furnished to each fully accredited Local Preacher in the following form:—

"A———B——— is a fully accredited Local Preacher, and is authorized to exercise the duties of this office in accordance with our Rules.

Signed<br>
C————D————<br>
Superintendent of E———Circuit."

Date

Printed copies of such forms may be obtained from the Secretary of the Conference.

**140** At one meeting of the year there shall be a conversation on the subject of personal religious experience, and on the best means of promoting the mental improvement and general efficiency of the brethren.

**141** The Local Preachers' Meeting may make such general arrangements for the direction of the work of its members as may seem expedient and necessary, and as shall not be inconsistent with these rules, or with Methodist usage in Ireland.

**142** It shall at any time be competent to the Quarterly Meeting to make such suggestions to the Local Preachers' Meeting for carrying on the work of God as may seem to it desirable; and in Circuits where no Local Preachers' Meeting can be held, the Quarterly Meeting shall possess the powers conferred in these rules on Local Preachers' Meetings.

# CHAPTER V.
# THE CONFERENCE.

### I. THE LEGAL CONFERENCE.

**143** During the early years of Methodism Mr. Wesley was accustomed to meet with the preachers under his care from year to year in England and Ireland, to confer with them as to the best methods of carrying on the work of God, and of " spreading Scriptural holiness throughout the land." At these Conferences the Preachers received their appointments for the year; new labourers were examined and approved; various funds were administered; and arrangements were made for the building of chapels, and the general advancement of the work of God. Wesley himself presided at these Conferences, and the entire direction was in his hands. The Conference had no legal status apart from him. Acting under legal advice, in 1784 he executed an instrument known as the Deed Poll, constituting one hundred Preachers the Conference of the people called Methodists; and providing that after the decease of himself and his brother Charles, the vacancies caused by death or otherwise should be filled up from the ranks of the Travelling Preachers from year to year. To this Conference Mr. Wesley transferred the power which he had exercised as to the acceptance, appointment, and expulsion of preachers, together with every other power which had centred in him. This deed was executed on the 28th of February, 1784, and afterwards enrolled in His Majesty's High Court of Chancery.

**144** Vacancies in the Legal Conference are caused

by death, by absence from the Conference for two successive years without a dispensation, and by the act of the Conference affirming that certain persons are no longer members of that body.

**145** With regard to the filling up of vacancies, the only requirement of the Deed of Declaration is, that "no person shall be elected a member of the Conference, who hath not been admitted into connexion with the Conference as a Preacher and expounder of God's Holy Word for twelve months." But the Conference has restricted the choice to Ministers who have travelled at least fourteen years, and has established the following mode of procedure. The Legal Conference having associated with itself during its Pastoral Session, all the Ministers in Full Connexion who have permission from their respective District Meetings to attend its sittings, it has been arranged that every alternate vacancy in the Legal Conference should be filled up by election after *nomination*. It is open to any member of the Conference to name any Minister who has travelled *fourteen* years, as specially eligible for this position; and then all Ministers who have travelled *ten* years and upwards are at liberty to vote in writing for any one of the persons so named, or for any other Minister who has travelled *fourteen* years. The Legal Conference is requested to elect the person who is nominated by the greatest number, which it does by a separate vote. The alternate vacancies are filled up by ballot by the Legal Conference from a list of Ministers in the full work, made out according to seniority.

**146** The chief powers confided to the Conference by the Deed of Declaration relate to the admission of persons to be "Preachers and expounders of God's Holy Word," or upon trial for this office, in connexion with the Conference; the putting out of any member of the Legal Conference from being a member thereof, and of any person admitted as a preacher into connexion with it, or upon trial, "for any cause which to the Conference may seem fit or necessary;" and the appointment of preachers "to the use and enjoyment of, or to preach and expound God's Holy Word in, any of the Chapels" of the Connexion.

**147** The thirteenth clause of this Deed gives the power to the Conference to appoint a Delegate or Delegates to hold a Conference in Ireland "when and as often as it shall seem expedient;" such Delegate or Delegates to have all, or any of, the powers which the Conference itself possesses. The clause reads as follows:—

"And for the convenience of the Chapels and premises already or which may hereafter be given or conveyed upon the trusts aforesaid, situate in Ireland or other parts out of the Kingdom of Great Britain, the Conference shall and may when and as often as it shall seem expedient, but not otherwise, appoint and delegate any member or members of the Conference with all or any of the powers, privileges and advantages hereinbefore contained or vested in the Conference; and all and every the acts, admissions, expulsions, and appointments whatsoever of such member or members of the Conference, so appointed and delegated as aforesaid, the same being put into writing, and signed by such Delegate or Delegates, and entered in the Journals or Minutes of the Conference, and subscribed as after mentioned, shall be deemed, taken, and be the acts, admissions, expulsions, and appointments of the Conference, to all intents, constructions, and purposes whatsoever, from the respective times when the same shall be done by such Delegate or Delegates, notwithstanding anything herein contained to the contrary."

**148** In accordance with the provisions contained in this clause, the Conference each year appoints its President, and in the case of his unavoidable absence, the Ex-President, or the member of the Irish proportion of the "Hundred" nominated by the Irish Conference, to be its Delegate in Ireland, and the following resolution is annually adopted and printed in the Minutes:—"The President or other Minister acting as Delegate under the authority of the preceding appointment, who shall preside at the next Conference in Ireland, shall exercise the powers confided to him under and by virtue of the thirteenth clause of Mr Wesley's Deed Poll, dated the 28th of February, 1784."

149  Ten members of the "Hundred" constituting the Legal Conference are uniformly members of the Irish Conference. When a vacancy occurs among these, the Irish Conference nominates the successor; and the Legal Conference is requested to elect the person so nominated. The rules governing the filling up of vacancies are the same as in the British Conference; (See par. 145;) except that all the members of the Conference, of *ten* years standing and upwards, are at liberty to vote in the case of those to be elected from the *senior* Ministers in the full work, as well as in the case of those who are elected *after nomination*. The member of the "Hundred," who is from year to year nominated by the Irish Conference for the position of "Delegate" is *ex-officio* the senior Representative to the British Conference and the Vice-President of the Irish Conference for the year.

## II. THE IRISH CONFERENCE.

150  Up to, and including, the year 1876, the Irish Conference consisted exclusively of Ministers who were in Full Connexion, and who had leave from their respective District Meetings to attend. In 1876 the Conference resolved upon an important alteration in its Constitution, whereby an adequate

and efficient representation of the Laity in the business of the Conference might be thereafter secured; a plan for carrying this into effect was adopted by the Conference of 1876, and the succeeding Conference was constituted in accordance with the provisions of that plan.

### 1. *Constitution.*

151  The Irish Conference as now constituted consists of two sessions, namely, a *Ministerial* Session and a *Representative* Session. For the consideration and determination of all business of the first named Session, the Conference consists of Ministers only; for the consideration and determination of all business of the second Session, the Conference consists of Ministers and Laymen in equal numbers.

152  The *Ministerial* Session consists—

1. Of the following, who are Members *Ex-Officio:*—

(1). The President.

(2). The members of the Irish proportion of the Legal Conference.

(3). The Secretary and the Assistant Secretaries of the preceding Irish Conference.

(4). The Representatives to the preceding British Conference.

(5). The Chairmen and the Financial Secretaries of Districts.

(6). The Ministerial Treasurers and Secretaries of the Connexional Funds and Committees.

(7). The President and the Theological Tutor of the Methodist College, and the Governor of Wesley College.

2. Of the Ministers elected according to Rule (see par. 156) by the several District Meetings to be members of the Conference in its Representative Session.

3. Of such other Ministers in Full Connexion as have permission from their District Meetings to attend.

153 The number of Ministers composing the Conference in its Ministerial Session shall be determined by the preceding Conference in its Ministerial Session, from year to year, according to circumstances, and the total number apportioned among the Districts.

154 The *Representative* Session consists—

1. Of the *Ex-Officio* Members of the Ministerial Session of the Conference.

2. Of Ministers elected in the respective District Meetings by the united votes of Ministers in Full Connexion and of the Lay members of the District Meeting in attendance. (See Chapter on District Meetings as to the Lay members of the Meeting.)

3. Of the Lay Treasurers of Connexional Funds.

4. Of Laymen chosen by Committees of Funds and Institutions; viz., four by the General Committee of Management, and one each by the Governors of the Methodist College, the Committee of Management of Wesley College, the Committee of the Hibernian Auxiliary to the Wesleyan Methodist Missionary Society, the Committee of the Orphan Fund, the Sunday School Committee, and the Temperance Committee.

5. Of Lay Representatives of the several Districts chosen by ballot from among gentlemen nominated as hereinafter provided; (see par. 160;) such election shall be by the united votes of Ministers in Full Connexion, and of the Laymen in attendance.

155 The proportion of Lay Representatives to be elected by each District Meeting shall be determined by the preceding Conference in its Representative Session, provided that the total number of *Elected* and *Ex-Officio* Lay members shall be equal to, and shall not exceed, the total number of Ministers.

## 2. *Rules affecting Elections.*

**156** In the election of Ministers in the District Meetings it is a condition that two Ministers in the full work on the same Circuit shall not be members of the Representative Session of the Conference, unless there be either an *Ex-Officio* or an *Elected* Representative from each Circuit on the District; and it is further provided that no Circuit on the District shall be left without a Ministerial Representative for more than two years in succession.

**157** In the election of Lay members of the Conference the District Meetings shall have priority of choice; the Committees of Management making their selection at meetings to be held after the District Meetings, in order to avoid a double election.

**158** The election by the Committees of Management shall be from among their own members, except in the case of the General Committee of Management in the special circumstances hereinafter provided for. (See section on General Committee of Management, par. 188.)

**159** When any vacancy occurs in the membership of the Conference in its Representative Session by the death of an *Ex-Officio* Member, in the interval between one Conference and another, the Committee to which such *Ex-Officio* Member stood related shall elect a Representative in his place.

**160** The election of Lay Representatives by the District Meetings shall be from persons nominated by the March Quarterly Meetings of the several Circuits of the District; such nominations shall be subject to the following conditions:

1. No one shall be eligible for nomination or election who is not twenty-five years of age, and who has not been, immediately preceding his nomination, a member of Society for, at least, five years consecutively.

2. Circuits having less than 200 members shall have the right of one nomination; Circuits having 200 and less than 400 shall have the right of two nominations; Circuits having 400 members and upwards shall have the right of three nominations. The number of members shall be taken as returned in the Minutes of the previous Conference.

3. Quarterly Meetings may nominate any eligible person, or persons, resident in the District to which the Circuit belongs.

4. If in any case the total number nominated by the Quarterly Meetings shall be less than the number to be elected by the District, then it shall be competent for the District Meeting to proceed to the nomination and appointment of the number required.

161 In connection with the names of Laymen on the voting lists for the Districts it shall be shown by what Circuits they were nominated, and also whether the nominees of such Circuits were elected the preceding year, so as to give the District Meeting an opportunity of securing that each Circuit on the District shall have from time to time, a fair share in the representation.

162 The names of two Ministerial and two Lay Members voted for at the May District Meeting, next in order of voting to those elected, shall be sent forward from each District as a Supplemental List (except in the case of Dublin and Belfast Districts, where the number shall be four Ministerial and four Lay Members); and in the event of any Representative, within twenty one days from his election, signifying to the Secretary of the Conference his inability to attend, the Secretary is empowered to take the name first in order on the Supplemental List of the District to which such Representative belongs, to supply his place.

E

### 3. *Arrangement of Business.*

**163** The Business of the Conference in its *Ministerial* Session shall include :—

1. Appointment of the Officers of Conference.
2. Nomination of Ministers to fill up vacancies in the Irish proportion of the Legal Conference. (For rules regulating nomination, see pars. 145 and 149.)
3. Admission of Preachers into Full Connexion, Continuance of Preachers on Trial, and Acceptance of Candidates.
4. All questions affecting Ministerial Character and competency for the work of the Ministry, and all appeals on matters of discipline relating either to Ministers or Members.
5. The character of Ministers who have died.
6. All questions relating to Ministers becoming Supernumerary, and also Ministers who are Supernumerary resuming full Ministerial Work.
7. Stations.
8. Election of Representatives to the British and other Conferences.
9. The Pastoral Address, and Addresses to the British and other Conferences.

**164** The following are the regulations affecting the election of Representatives to the British Conference. :—

1. The Minister chosen as the Vice-President for the year is the Senior Representative. (See par. 149.)
2. The second Representative shall be elected, after nomination, by the ballot of the Ministers in Full Connexion attending the Conference, from the Ministers who have travelled twenty years and upwards, and who are not members of the Legal Conference.
3. The third, or junior Representative shall be chosen in like manner from the Ministers in Full Connexion who have travelled more than ten and less than twenty years.

4. A clear majority of those present and voting is necessary in each case to a valid election.

**165** The Business of the Conference in its *Representative* Session shall include:—

1. Reports of Committees of Management of Connexional Funds and Institutions, with such general questions as affect them; and Reports of other Mixed Committees.
2. Appointments of all such Committees and their Officers, except where such appointments involve any question of Stations.
3. Statistics.
4. Alteration or Division of Circuits.
5. Increase or Diminution of the number of Ministers.
6. Public Questions affecting our Civil and Religious Privileges.

### 4. *General Rules of Procedure.*

**166** Every resolution proposed for discussion and adoption by the Conference shall, before it is admitted for discussion, be presented in writing to the President.

**167** No discussion shall take place on any resolution or Memorial proposing a change in the Constitution of the Body except after twelve months' notice of such resolution or Memorial given in writing.

**168** Suggestions from District Meetings and Memorials shall be considered by the Ministerial or by the Representative Session of the Conference according to their subject matter. If it be doubtful whether any question which arises shall be considered a purely Ministerial question or otherwise, the decision of the President for the time being shall determine.

**169** In all business relating to matters of administration, a majority of those present and voting shall be sufficient to decide any question; but for all *new* Laws, Rules, and Regulations which may, from time to time, be proposed, a majority of *two-thirds* of those present and voting shall be necessary before such measure shall be declared to be carried.

**170** In the case of a new appointment to any office relating to any of the Connexional Funds the names of, at least, three eligible persons shall be submitted to the Conference by the Committee in charge of the Fund.

**171** A Memorial may be addressed to the Conference by any individual member of the Methodist Church, on any subject affecting the personal church relations or interests of the Memorialist. Such Memorial must be forwarded to the Secretary of the Conference before the 12th of June, except in cases where the circumstances which occasion the Memorial arise after that date and before the sittings of the Conference.

(For the rules regulating Memorials from Quarterly Meetings see the section on Quarterly Meetings, par 233).

**172** Visitors shall be permitted to be present during the Sessions of the Representative Conference, except at such times as the Conference shall otherwise determine, and subject to the regulations hereinafter specified.

The gallery of the Conference Chapel shall be set apart for the accommodation of visitors. In addition to the Members of the Ministerial Conference who are not Representatives and who shall be admitted on showing their Conference tickets, Members of the Conference shall have power to admit visitors by giving to each a ticket in which the name of the visitor shall be written, and which shall be signed by the Member so admitting.

### III. OFFICERS OF THE CONFERENCE.

**173** *The President.*—The first Minister who presided in the Irish Conference after the death of Mr. Wesley was the Rev. Dr. Coke, and he thus explained the extent of the power which he supposed to be invested in him:—

1. "The President regulates all debates, but should not insist on any debates being brought to a conclusion without the leave of the Conference.

2. The President should have two votes if he please to exercise the privilege.

3. The Conference alone should determine the duration and time of its sittings, and the time of final conclusion.

4. Nothing should be determined but by the vote of the majority of the Conference."

The above regulations have been acted upon up to the present time.

The arrangement now existing is that the Minister appointed as "Delegate in Ireland" of the Legal Conference, is the President of the ensuing Irish Conference.

174 *The Vice-President of the Conference.* The term *Vice-President* has been chosen by the Irish Conference as the Official designation of the Member of the Irish proportion of the "Hundred" who is annually nominated to the position of "Delegate." (See pars. 148, 149.)

The same Minister shall not be appointed Vice-President two years in succession.

175 The powers and privileges of the President are, during the intervals of the Conference Sessions, vested in the Vice-President. To him all applications for supplies for Circuits from the List of Reserve must be made through the Chairmen of the respective Districts. He is the *ex-officio* Chairman of all Connexional Committees of which he is a member; and all questions arising in the course of the year which would be referred to the President if he were resident in Ireland, are to be referred to the Vice-President.

176 In case of the death of the Vice-President during the year, the last surviving Vice-President shall immediately enter again into the office so vacated; and shall be considered

for the remainder of the year, and until the appointment of a successor, as having all the powers, privileges, and authority of the Vice-President, and as responsible for all his duties. In case of the *severe* and *continued* illness of the Vice-President, the preceding regulation shall apply for the time, and to the extent which may be necessary.

177 *The Secretary of the Conference* is elected by the ballot of the Conference during its Ministerial Session. He is responsible for bringing up the business of the Conference in the order which may be agreed on, and for having a correct record made of the proceedings of the Conference. He is responsible also for the accuracy of the printed Minutes, as a record of the decisions of the Conference on the subjects to which they relate. It is also the duty of the Secretary to prepare and forward a copy of the "Acts of the Delegate in Ireland," embracing the "admissions, expulsions, and appointments" which, in accordance with the provisions of the Deed Poll, have to be recorded in the Journals of the Legal Conference.

178 *The Assistant Secretaries* are appointed by the vote of the Conference in its Ministerial Session.

### IV. THE STATIONING COMMITTEE.

179 The Stationing Committee is a Committee of the Conference, constituted as hereafter specified for the purpose of preparing and submitting to the Conference in its Ministerial Session a draft of the stations and appointments of the Ministers for the ensuing year, in accordance with the Rules affecting the Itinerancy.

180 The Stationing Committee consists of the President, the Vice-President, and the Secretary of the Conference, and the General Secretary of the Home Mission and Contingent Fund, together with one Minister from each District in Ireland.

N.B. The Assistant Secretaries of the Conference are directed to attend the Meetings of the Stationing Committee, to assist in preparing the necessary lists for the use of the Conference.

181 The District Representatives to the Stationing Committee shall be elected in the Annual District Meetings by the united votes of Ministers and Laymen, and shall be chosen out of the Ministers previously elected to be Members of the Conference in its Representative Session.

182 The Stationing Committee is authorized to act upon the recommendations of the District Meetings with regard to Ministers becoming Supernumerary.

(For further rules affecting the action of the Stationing Committee, see Section on the "The Itinerancy" par. 106-110).

### V. THE GENERAL COMMITTEE OF MANAGEMENT.

#### 1. *Origin and Design.*

183 The General Committee of Management is a Committee of the Representative Session of the Conference. It was first constituted in 1878. The object of its appointment was to bring various Connexional Funds, having a close relation to each other, under one general oversight and management. These funds had previously been managed by separate Committees, but this was found, for several reasons, inconvenient; and it was resolved by the Conference, while maintaining the distinct appropriation of the funds as formerly, to unite the Managing Committees in one General Committee for these departments.

#### 2 *Constitution and Business.*

184 The General Committee of Management shall consist of the Vice-President of the Conference, (who shall be Chairman of the Committee) the Secretary of the Conference, the Treasurers and the Secretaries of the Home Mission

and Contingent Fund, the Supernumerary Ministers' and Ministers' Widows' Fund, the Chapel Fund, the General Education Fund, the Children's Fund, and the Registrar of Connexional Deeds; together with eleven Ministers and eighteen Laymen to be elected by ballot of the Conference from those Ministers and Laymen who are, at the time of their election, Members of the Conference, provided that in the result of such ballot there shall be at least one Minister and one Layman elected from each District.

185 Two ordinary meetings of the Committee shall be held in each year, one beginning on the second Tuesday in September, and the other on the third Tuesday in May, but it shall be at all times competent for the Vice-President of the Conference, if occasion shall arise which seems to him to require that the ordinary time of meeting should be altered, or that more than two meetings should be held during the year, to direct that the Committee be convened accordingly.

186 The Secretary of the Conference shall be the Convener of the Committee; but the Secretaries of the several departments, the business of which is transacted by the Committee, shall each be responsible for bringing up in due form at the meetings of the Committee the business belonging to his own department; for preserving the records of the proceedings of the Committee in relation to such business; and for preparing such reports thereon as are to be presented to the Conference.

187 The Committee shall have the general oversight and management of the Home Mission and Contingent Fund, the Chapel Fund, the General Education Fund, the Children's Fund, and the Supernumerary Ministers' and Ministers' Widows' Fund; and shall have referred to it any applications which may be made, or questions which may arise in connection with the erection, purchase, alteration, sale, or proper

settlement of Ministers' residences, Chapels, School-houses, or other Trust Property. The Committee shall also consider any other business which from time to time the Conference may remit to it.

188  The Committee is empowered to elect at its meeting in May, four of its Lay Members to be members of the Conference in its Representative Session, provided that if in any case it appear at the meeting of the Committee prior to the Conference, that the selection of Representatives already made by the District Meetings and by other Committees of the Conference, has included so many Lay Members of the Managing Committee as to leave the Committee unable to appoint from among its own members the number allotted, without involving a double election, then it shall be competent for the Committee to proceed to the nomination and election of any eligible person or persons not members of the Committee, but who have been nominated by their respective Quarterly Meetings for election to the ensuing Conference, in order to complete the number required.

189  The Chairman and the Secretary of the Committee, the Officers of the Home Mission Fund, the Chapel Fund, and the Education Fund, together with the members of the General Committee of Management residing in the Dublin District, shall constitute a Sub-Committee, which shall have power to consider and deal with such matters of business relating to any of these departments as may arise in the intervals of the General Committee Meetings.

190  The Sub-Committee shall meet on the last Friday in every month. All communications should be sent to its Secretary at least two days before the monthly meeting.

191  The Secretary shall furnish to the several Secretaries of Funds, before the meeting of the General Committee in

May, an abstract of all cases belonging to their departments which have been considered during the year.

### VI. THE COMMITTEE OF PRIVILEGES.

192 The Committee of Privileges is a Committee of the Conference, consisting of equal numbers of Ministers and Lay Gentlemen, with the Vice-President and the Secretary of the Conference as *ex-officio* members, appointed annually by the Conference during its Representative Session, for the purpose of guarding the privileges of our Connexion in Ireland. All the Ministers who have filled the office of Vice-President together with the Treasurers and the Secretary of the General Education Fund, are also *ex-officio* members of the Committee.

193 The duty of the Committee is to consider all cases of exigency arising in any Department of the affairs of the Connexion, or otherwise, requiring prompt communication with the Government, or with Parliament, on subjects affecting our public interests; and to take such action as the circumstances may require. It is also the duty of the Committee to act on behalf of the Conference, during the intervals of its sittings, in any public Ceremonial in which the Methodist Church should be represented.

194 The Vice-President of the Conference shall have authority to direct the summoning of the Committee whenever he shall deem it necessary; and shall at any time, on receiving a requisition to that effect, signed by seven members of the Committee, be required to direct that the Committee shall be summoned for the consideration of the particular business specified in such requisition.

# CHAPTER VI.
## DISTRICT MEETINGS.

#### I. ORIGIN AND DESIGN.

**195** The division of the Connexion into Districts was a measure resolved upon at the first Conference held after the death of Mr Wesley, and was intended to meet cases of emergency which, during his life, had been submitted to his personal decision. But in the gradual development of Methodism, District Meetings have become most important parts of its economy; and the *Annual* and the *Financial District Meetings* in particular, are essential to the carrying out of the Connexional system.

**196** Every District Meeting is properly a Committee of the Conference; to which body its Minutes are to be presented, and its recommendations reported. The functions of the District Committee are usually to be regarded as strictly for *administration* in relation to the people, and for *recommendation* and *suggestion* in relation to the Conference.

#### II. ANNUAL DISTRICT MEETING.

**197** The Annual District Meeting is to be held, at the latest, in the first week in May. It is the duty of all Ministers and Preachers on Trial to attend its sittings, and no exemption from this regulation can be admitted, except in case of sickness or other equally reasonable cause.

Preachers on Trial, though required to attend the sittings of the Annual District Meeting, have not the right to vote in any of its proceedings.

**198** The business of the District Meeting is arranged under two general heads, viz.: 1, *Ministerial*; and 2, *Financial* *and General.* During the transaction of the Financial and General business, the Circuit Stewards of every Circuit within the bounds of the District are members of the District Meeting. If the Circuit Stewards are unable to attend, the Quarterly Meeting of the Circuit has the right to elect any of its own members to take their place in the Meeting, and to act on their behalf. The Lay Members of the District Chapel Sub-Committee are also to be regarded as members of the District Meeting when Chapel Affairs are under consideration ; and if there be a District Sunday School Union, the Secretary of the Union shall be admitted to the District Meeting during the discussion of educational business. Members of the General Committee of Management are *ex-officio* Members of the District Meeting of the District which they represent for the year.

199 The *Chairman* of each District is appointed in the Ministerial Session of the Conference by the vote, taken by ballot, of all the Ministers in Full Connexion who are present.

The Minister previously nominated as *Vice-President* of the Conference for the ensuing year, is *ex-officio* Chairman of the District in which he resides.

200 The *Secretaries* of Districts are appointed in like manner in the Ministerial Session of the Conference. They act not only as Secretaries of the Annual District Meeting, but as Financial Secretaries ; and through them is to be made at the Conference, the settlement of accounts between Superintendents of Circuits and the Treasurers of the several Funds.

*Assistant Secretaries* of Districts, when needed, are appointed by the District Meeting on the nomination of the Secretary.

NOTE—See "*Order and Form of Business for District Meetings,*" published by the direction of the Conference, for details of the business of District Meetings.

### III. FINANCIAL DISTRICT MEETING.

**201** The Financial District Meeting is to be held in the third week in August. It is not binding on all the Ministers of the District to be present, as in the case of the Annual District Meeting; but it is the duty of all Superintendents to attend, and the presence of as many other Ministers as can arrange to come is very desirable. The Circuit Stewards of each Circuit within the District are members of the Meeting during all its proceedings.

N.B. 1. The provision made to meet the case of the inability of the Circuit Stewards to attend the sittings of the Annual District Meeting, applies also to the Financial District Meeting (see par. 198).

2. See Note at the close of preceding paragraph.

### IV. THE MINOR DISTRICT MEETING.

**202** The Minor District Meeting is intended to afford a convenient and suitable method of investigating charges preferred against Ministers or Preachers on Trial, and of hearing appeals from the disciplinary proceedings of Leaders' Meetings, which otherwise must lie over till the meeting of the Annual District Committee.

**203** The Minor District Meeting shall consist of not less than five of the Ministers of the District, viz. the Chairman of the District and four other Ministers, two of whom shall be chosen by the person bringing the charge, and two by the person accused; in case either or both these parties should neglect or refuse to choose two Ministers to act as members of the Meeting, the Chairman is empowered and directed to make the choice.

**204** Before a Minor District Meeting is called to investigate any charge, the Chairman who receives it shall send to the person accused an exact statement in writing of the charge made against him, with the name of the person by whom the charge is preferred.

**205** Should the Chairman of the District himself be the person making the accusation, or the person accused, then the President of the Conference, or the Minister of the Irish Conference who fills the office of Vice-President for the year, shall act in this case as if he were the Chairman of the District in which the accused resides.

**206** In all ordinary cases, when the holding of a Minor District Meeting is rendered necessary, such meeting shall be held in the District in which the accused person resides; but if the matter of complaint have taken place in a different District, so as to render it difficult on account of great distance, to secure the attendance of witnesses if the Minor District Meeting be held in the usual place, then the President or Vice-President for the time being, on the case being represented to him, shall have power to direct the Chairman of the District in which the cause of complaint arose, to investigate the matter in a Minor District Meeting of that District. The proceedings of every Minor District Meeting, so held shall be fully reported to the Chairman of the District in which the accused is stationed, or to the Conference if the proceedings have taken place in the interval between the District Meeting and the Conference.

**207** In all cases when the accuser or the person accused is dissatisfied with the decision of the Minor District Meeting, there shall be the right of appeal to the Annual District Meeting, and the right also of further or final appeal to the Conference. In case of an appeal to the Annual District Meeting, it shall be to that District Meeting to which the Members of the Minor District Meeting belong. If the Minor District Meeting has been held between the

Annual District Meeting and the Conference, then any appea which may be taken shall be to the Conference.

**208** The Annual District Meeting is bound to review the proceedings of any Minor District Meeting which may have been held before it assembles, and to record its judgment thereon. In cases of appeal, whether from a Minor District Meeting to the Annual District Meeting, or from either or both to the Conference, notice must be given to the Chairman of the District.

### V. DUTIES OF CHAIRMEN OF DISTRICTS.

**209** It is the duty of the Chairman of a District to fix the time and place for the holding of the District Meeting, (unless the place has been fixed either by usage, or by the vote of a previous Meeting,) to preside over its deliberations, and to see that the ordinary and special business to be transacted is brought forward in due order.

**210** Each Chairman is authorized to visit officially any Circuit in his District to which he shall be invited by the Superintendent; or respecting which after consultation with the Superintendent, he shall be satisfied that his intervention may be serviceable to the preservation of peace and order, or to the faithful and judicious execution of our discipline, or administration of our economy.

**211** The Chairmen of Districts are directed to visit each Circuit in their respective Districts to which only one Minister is appointed, at least once in each year wherever it is at all practicable, and if possible at the time of holding a Quarterly Meeting.

**212** In such cases as the August District Meeting may deem necessary, the Chairman of the District, or some one deputed by him shall, in the course of the year, visit one Quarterly

Meeting of each claimant Circuit in order to assist by his counsel such Circuit in attaining a self-supporting position.

**213** It is the duty of the Chairman to examine the Lists of Removals and Receptions of Members within his District as prescribed by the Rules relating to this subject (see par. 8).

NOTE—For other duties of Chairmen of Districts see Chapters on "The Home Mission and Contingent Fund," "The Chapel Fund," and "The General Education Fund."

### VI. DUTIES OF SECRETARIES OF DISTRICTS.

**214** It is the duty of the Secretary, under the directions of the Chairman, to inform the members of the District Committee as to the time and place of holding the meeting. He is to inform the Circuit Stewards as well as the Ministers, and, in order to this, the Superintendents of Circuits are directed to give him the names and addresses of their respective Circuit Stewards, or of the Members of the Quarterly Meeting deputed to take their place (see par. 198) immediately after the March Quarterly Meeting.

**215** The Secretary is to prepare lists of Ministers, and of the Lay-gentlemen who have been nominated by the Quarterly Meetings, from which the District Committee is to elect the allotted number of Representatives to the ensuing Conference.

**216** The Secretary, in addition to the entry of minutes of proceedings in the District Book is to provide two complete copies of the Minutes of the Annual District Meeting, and one copy of the Minutes of the Financial District Meeting, written on foolscap paper, and duly signed by the Chairman and Secretary. One copy of the Minutes of the Annual District Meeting shall be reserved for the use of the Chairman and the other copy, together with the copy of the Minutes of the Financial District Meeting, shall be forwarded to the

Secretary of the Conference, as may be directed from time to time.

217  It is also the duty of the Secretary to see that all "Returns" which are directed to be forwarded to the Officers of the several departments, or to the Secretary or Assistant Secretaries of the Conference, are forwarded in due time. Any official "Forms" sent to the District Meeting for the use of the Superintendents are also to be distributed by the Secretary, or by some one on his behalf.

# CHAPTER VII.

# LOCAL OFFICERS AND MEETINGS.

### I. LEADERS AND LEADERS' MEETINGS.

#### 1. *Leaders.*

218 The duties of a Leader, in the original constitution of the Methodist Society, are set forth in the "General Rules," (see pp. 3 and 4,) and this summary of duties must still be regarded as of binding obligation on all who sustain this office. The only particular in which the original rule has been superseded by general usage is that in which the Leader is required "to meet the Ministers and Stewards of the Society *once a week*." Such meetings are now rarely held oftener than *once a month*; but, whenever held, it is the duty of the Leader to be present. And, whether at the Meeting or in the interval between one meeting and another, it is important and obligatory that the Leader should inform the Minister of those Members who are sick, or require to be specially visited.

Let it be observed that no Leader has power to put any person either into or out of the Society.

219 No person shall be appointed to the office of Leader or removed from his office, without the approbation of a Leaders' Meeting, where such meeting can be obtained. The nomination of the Leader is with the Superintendent.

Whenever it shall appear practicable, especially in the old and large societies, some active, zealous men whose piety and general character are approved by the Leaders' Meetings, should be appointed to attempt the formation of new Classes in suitable neighbourhoods, where there is reason to hope persons may be gathered into the fold of Christ who are not far from the Kingdom of God, but who need special invitation and are not likely to "give themselves" fully "to the Lord and to us by the will of God" without more than ordinary labour and spiritual attention.

220 As much depends, under the blessing of God, on the piety, knowledge, zeal, activity, and Christian temper of our Leaders, as well as on their firm attachment to the doctrines, discipline and cause of Methodism, no Superintendent should ever nominate a new Leader until he has conscientiously satisfied himself by previous inquiry and personal examination, as to the character of the person proposed; and the rule respecting the public examination of Leaders, when one is first introduced into the meeting, should be uniformly observed.

2. *The Leaders' Meeting.*

221 The Leaders' Meeting shall consist of (1) the Ministers and Preachers on Trial who are appointed to the work of the Circuit; (2) the Supernumerary or other Ministers resident within the bounds of that Society; (3) the Leaders of the Society, the Society Stewards, of whom there shall not be more than two, the Stewards of the Poor's Fund, and any Circuit Steward or Stewards who may be members of that Society.

222 No person shall be appointed a Society Steward, or Poor Steward, but in conjunction with a Leaders' Meeting; the nomination to be with the Superintendent, and the approval or disapproval with the Leaders' Meeting.

223 It is the duty of the *Society Stewards* to attend the Leaders' Meeting of the Society, to receive the money contributed in the classes towards the support of the Ministry, to

take charge of the Sabbath Collections, to defray any local charges which may arise in connection with the maintenance of public worship, and to account quarterly with the Circuit Stewards.

224 In Circuits where, though there may be two or more congregations, there is but one Leaders' Meeting, Chapel Stewards may be appointed instead of Society Stewards, for other than the principal Chapel on the Circuit; they are appointed under the same Rule, and have the same duties as Society Stewards, as far as practicable.

225 The Stewards of the Poor's Fund receive the collections made on behalf of the Poor at the Lord's Supper, and at the Love Feasts. They provide the bread and wine for the Sacrament of the Lord's Supper, and the bread and water for the Love Feasts. They attend the Leaders' Meeting to pay any sums that may be voted for the poor members of the Society.

226 The *Secretary* of a Leaders' Meeting, if one is appointed, must be chosen from among the members of the Meeting.

## II. CIRCUIT STEWARDS AND QUARTERLY MEETINGS.

### 1. *Circuit Stewards.*

227 Circuit Stewards are appointed or re-appointed at the December Quarterly Meeting of the Circuit; the nomination being with the Superintendent, and the approval or disapproval with the Quarterly Meeting.

As a general rule Circuit Stewards shall not be appointed to office for more than three years in succession; but in special circumstances, the Superintendent may, if he think fit, nominate, and the Quarterly Meeting may appoint for a longer period.

223 The ordinary duties of a Circuit Steward are:—

1. To receive the contributions from the various Societies on the Circuit, and from all other sources, on behalf of the support of the Ministers appointed to the Circuit by the Conference.

2. To pay in full the stipend of the Minister, *at least quarterly*.

3. To pay Minister's House-rent and Taxes.

4. To keep the Circuit Accounts in the book provided for that purpose.

5. To account Quarterly with the Superintendent for one fourth of the sum charged upon each Circuit, as its proportion of the Connexional Assessment for the year.

6. To sign any petition for the appointment of a Minister or Ministers to the Circuit, which shall be agreed to at the Quarterly Meeting.

7. To attend the District Meetings while the Financial concerns of the District are considered, and to take part in the proceedings and vote.

## 2. *Quarterly Meetings.*

229 The Quarterly Meeting consists of:

1. All the Ministers and Preachers on trial in the Circuit, and the Supernumeraries whose names appear in the printed Minutes of the Conference. 2. The Circuit Stewards, the Society Stewards, the Chapel Stewards and the Stewards of the Poor's Fund. 3. All the Class Leaders in the Circuit. 4. All the Local Preachers of three years continuous standing, after having been twelve months on trial, they being resident Members of Society in the Circuit. 5. All the Trustees of Chapels situated in places named on the Circuit Plan; such Trustees being resident Members of Society in the Circuit. 6. When the Pew Steward is a member of Society, and

resident in the Circuit, he shall be a Member of the Quarterly Meeting. 7. When a Superintendent of a Sunday School being a Member of Society, resident in the Circuit, has been duly appointed by the Quarterly Meeting, on the nomination of the Superintendent Minister, he shall be a Member of the Quarterly Meeting. No Sunday School shall have more than one representative in the Quarterly Meeting.

**230** The Superintendent of the Circuit presides at the Quarterly Meeting. In the unavoidable absence of the Superintendent from the Quarterly Meeting, a Colleague in Full Connexion shall preside; or if there be no such Colleague the chair shall be occupied by the Chairman of the District.

**231** The ordinary *Business* of the Quarterly Meeting is

1. To receive from the Stewards a statement of Circuit income and expenditure.

2. To allocate amount of Poor's Fund.

3. To enquire as to amounts raised for Connexional Funds, and as to remittances to the several Treasurers.

4. To examine into the state of the work of God in the Circuit, and to adopt means of promoting it.

5. To enquire into the state of the Trust Property, Deeds, and number of Trustees. (See par. 232.)

6. To nominate persons to the Annual District Meeting, eligible for election as Representatives to Conference.

7. To approve of young men recommended by the Superintendent as Candidates for the Ministry, who have been full and accredited Local Preachers, and if otherwise considered suitable. (See par. 67.)

8. To recommend, if deemed advisable, the alteration or division of the Circuit.

9. To apply for permission of General Committee of Management, through the District Meeting, or District Chapel sub-Committee, for the erection, purchase, or enlarge-

ment of any Chapel, Minister's residence or other Trust Property that the meeting may consider necessary.

10. To sanction any application for grants from Home Mission, General Education, or Chapel Funds.

11. To examine into the state of the Sunday Schools, Day Schools, and Temperance Organizations on the Circuit.

12. To make application on behalf of children who are considered eligible to be taken under the care of the Orphan Society.

13 To request the Conference to appoint to the Circuit such Minister or Ministers as the meeting may consider suitable. (See pars. 106—108.)

14. To discharge the duties devolving on Trustees in cases where it is not practicable to hold regular Trustees' Meetings. (See pars. 236—243.)

15. To transact whatever business is considered necessary in the interests of the Circuit. (For details of Business see "*Order and Form of Business of Quarterly Meetings*," published by direction of the Conference.)

232 A Schedule of Trust Property on the Circuit, showing the condition of each Trust as to debt, state of repair, and other particulars compiled from the Annual Reports of the Trustees (see par. 237) shall be submitted to the March Quarterly Meeting in each year and afterwards forwarded to the District Chapel Secretary. In the case of loans from the Board of Public Works, under the provisions of the "Glebes Loans Act," for any Minister's Residence, the entire amount borrowed shall be stated in the Schedule, together with the number of half-yearly instalments paid.

233 The following are the Rules with regard to the adoption and forwarding of MEMORIALS from Quarterly Meetings to the Conference:—

1. When a majority of the March or June Quarterly Meet-

ing in any Circuit is of opinion that it is desirable to address to the Conference a memorial on any Connexional subject, and agrees to do so, the meeting has authority to adopt and transmit to the Conference such a Memorial; and at such meeting any member thereof may propose for consideration the propriety of addressing a Memorial to the Conference.

2. Previously to the day appointed for the holding of the March or June Quarterly Meeting, a copy, in writing, must be given to the Superintendent, of the particular motion or resolution which any member of the Quarterly Meeting intends to propose as the basis of a Memorial to the Conference; and the Superintendent shall read this document to the meeting at an early period of its sitting. If the Quarterly Meeting adopts the substance or principle of a resolution so brought forward, it can amend as well as simply adopt it; but no proposal of which such notice has not been given can be brought forward that year.

3. A memorial founded on such motion or resolution, if approved by a majority of the persons present, must set forth in its preamble the names of those in attendance at the meeting, and must be signed, within a week afterwards, by such of them as have voted in favour of it. It shall then remain with the Superintendent, who shall be responsible for its transmission to the Secretary of the Conference not later than the 12th of June following.

N.B.—The foregoing regulations do not apply to resolutions of Quarterly Meetings passed in the ordinary course of business with reference to Circuit affairs.

(For the rule relating to Memorials from individual Members of the Church, see par. 171.)

234 If it be deemed expedient for any cause to adjourn the Quarterly Meeting, and that a majority of those present and voting are in favour of adopting this course, such adjourn-

ment shall take place to some convenient time not later than that day four weeks.

### III. TRUSTEES AND TRUSTEES' MEETINGS.

235 It is the Rule of the Connexion that no person shall be appointed a Trustee of any Connexional Trust Property who is not a Member of Society.

236 The Superintendent of the Circuit is, *ex-officio*, Chairman of the Trustees' Meeting.

Trustees are bound to take care that the use of Church Property is restricted religiously to Church uses, in accordance with the provisions of the Trust Deed of the premises.

237 Where practicable, a Meeting of Trustees shall be held, at least, once in every year at which the Annual Accounts of the Trust shall be audited and the result reported to the Circuit Quarterly Meeting. Minutes of all such meetings should be taken and preserved.

238 The Trustees' Meeting may appoint a suitable person to be the Pew Steward, whose duty it shall be to look after the proper letting of Pews and "Sittings," to collect the pew rents, and to account for the same at the Trustees' Meeting, or at the Quarterly Meeting, as he may be directed.

239 The income derivable from pew rents, or from annual collections on behalf of the Trust, or from other sources, is to be applied :—(1) to the discharge of liabilities incurred for rent or interest on debt, &c. (2) to the maintenance of the Trust premises in proper repair; (3) to the Circuit Funds.

240 As it may sometimes be found that a sufficient number of Trustees are not resident within such a distance as to make it practicable to hold regular Trustees' Meetings ; in such cases the duties of the Trustees' Meeting shall devolve upon the Circuit Quarterly Meeting ; provided always that

nothing is done, or allowed, which is inconsistent with the provisions of the Trust Deed and that no new liability is incurred without the consent of the Trustees.

241 As it is of the utmost importance that the property held in Trust for the use of the Methodist Societies or of the Methodist Ministers and their families, in the several Circuits of the Connexion should not only be carefully applied to its destined purpose, but should be maintained in a proper state of fitness, the Conference earnestly urges the matter upon the consideration of all Trustees, Stewards, and Ministers, and expresses the hope that they will heartily co-operate in any measures which may be necessary towards this end.

242 As much damage to buildings may arise for want of a little timely outlay in necessary renovations, or repairs, the Conference directs all Superintendents of Circuits to see that the outlay needed for such purposes shall be brought under the consideration of the Trustees—or, if there be no acting body of Trustees, under the consideration of the Quarterly Meeting of the Circuit, or of the Leaders' Meeting of the particular Society with which the property is identified, and that there be no unnecessary delay in making the expenditure required.

It is to be regarded as a rule obligatory upon Trustees, or Stewards, or others having the care of Church buildings, or of Ministers' residences, that all external woodwork is to be repainted at least every four years, and all internal woodwork every six years.

243 If the necessary expenditure amounts to such a sum as requires the sanction of the District Committee and the General Committee of Management before it can be entered upon, the Superintendent of the Circuit, in conjunction with the Trustees, is directed promptly to take such steps as may be requisite in order to obtain such sanction,

**244** In the case of the renewal of old Trusts, when provision for the appointment of new Trustees is not made in the original Trust Deed, the selection shall be made by the Quarterly Meeting on the nomination of the Superintendent. In the case of new Trusts, Superintendents are required to submit a draft of the intended Trust Deed to the General Committee of Management for examination.

### IV. PRAYER LEADERS' MEETINGS.

**245** Whereas it has been found by long experience that public Prayer Meetings held in different parts of a town or neighbourhood, and at such times as do not interfere with general public worship, when prudently conducted by persons of established piety and competent gifts, have proved to be valuable nurseries for our Congregations and Societies, and means of salvation to many who could not have been reached at first by any other method, all Superintendents are directed to encourage such Meetings as much as is in their power; and in order to this, let there be in every Society, if possible, a recognized body of Prayer Leaders, and a regular Plan for the holding of Cottage Prayer Meetings.

**246** Let the Superintendent, or one of his colleagues meet the Prayer Leaders, at least, every quarter, to encourage them in their work, and to inquire into their attention to their appointments, the attendance at the Prayer Meetings, and into any spiritual good which may be known to have resulted from them.

**247** At these Meetings let the practicability and expediency of establishing additional Prayer Meetings be considered, and let the Plan for the ensuing quarter be prepared. Let also suitable persons be proposed for the office of Prayer Leader; and if they be appointed, let their names be submitted to the Leaders' Meeting for its approval in order to their being placed upon the Plan.

**248** Let it be observed, however, that it is a general rule of our Connexion that no person belonging to any other communion shall be appointed to a public office among us without the consent of the Conference being first obtained.

### V. SUNDAY SCHOOLS, TEACHERS, AND COMMITTEES.

**249** The main object of Methodist Sunday Schools shall be to instruct and train Scholars in the doctrines privileges, and duties of the Christian religion. The Holy Scriptures, and, as far as possible, the Methodist Catechisms shall be used as the means of such instruction and training. The Schools shall be conducted in distinct and avowed connection with the Methodist Society, and shall, in every practicable way, be worked in harmony with its arrangements, and with a view to its increase and benefit.

**250** Every Sunday School shall be under the management of a Committee consisting of (1) The Ministers of the Circuit; (2) the Superintendent and Officers of the School; and (3) the fully accredited Teachers. The Committee shall meet at least once a quarter.

**251** The Superintendent Minister of the Circuit shall preside in all meetings of the Committee, and of the Teachers, at which he may be present. In his absence the chair shall be taken by one of his colleagues; or, if no Minister be present, by the Superintendent of the School. All rules and regulations made for the School shall be subject to the approval of the Circuit Quarterly Meeting.

**252** The Officers of the School shall be as follows:—

1. A Superintendent, or Superintendents, to be annually appointed by the Circuit Quarterly Meeting on the nomination of the Chairman.

2. A Secretary and a Librarian, to be annually chosen by the Teachers' Meeting. All the Officers shall be selected from members of the Methodist Society.

253 The Teachers, whenever practicable, shall be members of the Methodist Society; but, if not, they must be regular attendants on the Methodist ministry, of good moral character, and heartily attached to the doctrines and discipline of Methodism. They may be received on trial by the Superintendent of the School; after a probation of three months they shall be nominated by him at a Teachers' meeting, and, if approved, elected by the meeting.

254 No person shall be continued as an Officer or Teacher who shall at any time be declared by the Committee, or by the Quarterly Meeting, unfit, in respect of general character, or religious opinions, for the office he sustains, or for taking part in the Christian education of the young.

255 Catechetical exercises shall form a constant part of the system of the School, and the Catechisms used shall be those published under the sanction of the Methodist Conference.

256 All the Scholars shall be trained to regular attendance on public worship on the Lord's day; and, wherever it is practicable, a select class or classes of those Scholars who are seriously disposed, shall be formed for special religious instruction and prayer, and shall be met in separate class-rooms on Sunday afternoon or on a week evening.

## VI. ASSOCIATIONS, ETC.

### 1. *Young Men's Associations, &c.*

257 It is a radical principle of our ecclesiastical polity that any institution claiming to be Methodist, or claiming the right to use any part or portion of Connexional Trust Property, must be under the supervision and direction of the Superintendent of the Circuit and the Circuit authorities.

258 As to the use of Church property for the accommodation of Young Men's Associations and similar institutions,

the Superintendent of the Circuit and the Trustees are bound to take care that such appropriation is restricted religiously to Church purposes, in accordance with the provisions of the Trust Deeds of the premises.

## 2. *Bands of Hope.*

**259** The Conference directs that in the formation and promotion of Bands of Hope in connection with our congregations, care shall be taken by the Ministers in charge and the friends interested, that they be brought into perfect harmony with the Methodist Constitution, and be placed under the supervision of the Superintendents of the Circuits, in conjunction with the Leaders' meetings.

# PART II.
FUNDS AND INSTITUTIONS.

# PART II.

## FUNDS AND INSTITUTIONS.

### CHAPTER I.

### CIRCUIT FINANCES.

#### 1. CIRCUIT INCOME.

260 It is a principle in Methodism that each Circuit is expected to take upon itself the responsibility of providing the funds necessary for the maintenance of its own Ministers, and for the incidental expenses connected with carrying on the work within the bounds of the Circuit; with the understanding, however, that feeble Circuits may receive assistance from the Home Mission and Contingent Fund, so long as the necessity is proved to exist.

261 The sources of Circuit Income are (1) Class money and Quarterage; (2) Sabbath Collections; (3) Special Collections in the Congregation on behalf of Circuit Funds; (4) Subscriptions or Donations from members of the Congregation or friends of the cause, given specifically in aid of the Circuit Funds; (5) Income derived from Pew Rents, after deducting necessary charges.

**262** Bequests are frequently made for the purpose of assisting in the support of the Ministry in connection with various Circuits or Congregations; when these bequests are intended to be invested, and the annual proceeds only applied for this purpose, the Board of Trustees appointed by the Conference is prepared to receive such bequests, and to see after the proper investment and due appropriation of the proceeds in accordance with the design of the testators. Superintendents of Circuits are requested to communicate full information to the Secretary of the Board of Trustees concerning all donations and bequests for Circuit or Connexional purposes, in connection with their Circuits.

**263** The Conference recommends that the Superintendents and their colleagues, with the affectionate co-operation of the Stewards and Leaders, shall prudently and legitimately employ such means as may improve the local income of their respective Circuits.

## II. CIRCUIT EXPENDITURE.

**264** The *ordinary* expenditure of a Circuit is of two classes; *first*, the *maintenance* of the *Ministers* and their families; and *second*, the *incidental expenses* arising from the Itinerancy, together with the *working expenses* of the Circuit.

**265** To the first-named class belong (1) the Stipends of the Ministers; (2) the rent and taxes payable on account of their residences; (3) the cost of providing and maintaining suitable furniture; and (4) the Assessment on behalf of the Children's Fund and the Supernumerary Ministers' and Ministers' Widows' Fund.

**266** To avoid the inconvenience and inequality which would necessarily arise under the system of an itinerant ministry, if each Circuit were directly responsible for the allowances made to its Ministers for the maintenance and education of their children, the Conference has directed that the Circuits shall be assessed in proportion to the number of Ministers (whether in full connexion or probationers) appointed to each Circuit, and out of the common fund thus created the allowances for children are paid. And as it is but equitable that Circuits should provide, to some extent, for Ministers who are worn out in their service, and for the widows of Ministers, the same arrangement has been made for this purpose, and Circuits are assessed in a certain annual amount in proportion to the number of Ministers stationed therein.

267 The Conference directs that the Circuit Stewards shall account quarterly with the Superintendents for one-fourth of the sum charged upon each Circuit as its proportion of the "Assessment" for the above-named purposes. Should this sum be more than the amount of the allowances payable to children of Ministers in the Circuit, the surplus shall be forwarded to the Treasurers of the Children's Fund not later than the first week in October, January, and April respectively, for the first three quarters, and through the District Financial Secretaries for the last quarter. Should the sum be less than the amount of such allowances, the Treasurers shall remit to the Superintendents the balance for the first three quarters and through the District Financial Secretaries for the last quarter.

268 To the class of *incidental* and *working expenses* belong (1) the expense incurred for travelling and carriage of luggage of the Minister and his family in removing to the Circuit; (2) the expense of travelling in the Circuit and to the District Meetings; (3) the allowance for postage and stationery made to the Superintendent of the Circuit; and

(4) the expense incurred for lighting, heating, and cleaning, the various Chapels or places of worship in the Circuit.

269 In addition to the *ordinary* expenditure of a Circuit, there may also be *extraordinary* expenditure occasioned by (1) lengthened and severe affliction in the Minister's family, or by (2) the providing a supply in case of the Minister's illness or death.

(For the conditions on which grants are made to assist in defraying the *Ordinary* or the *Extraordinary* expenditure of a Circuit, see the Chapter on the Home Mission and Contingent Fund.)

### III. CIRCUIT ACCOUNTS.

270 The Conference directs and requires Superintendents of Circuits to see to it that their Circuit Stewards keep accurate quarterly accounts of income and expenditure, and that as soon as possible after the close of the December Quarter, the Annual Statement of Income and Expenditure for the year then ending is made out and entered in its proper place in the Circuit Stewards' Book, and duly audited by Auditors appointed by the December Quarterly Meeting. The Conference recommends that the above-named Statement of Circuit Income and Expenditure be printed and distributed amongst the members of Society, and other contributors to the Circuit Funds.

271 The Conference imperatively directs that the published Circuit Stewards' Account Book shall be provided and kept in every dependent Circuit, and that the Chairmen of Districts shall enquire, in every case where a Circuit seeks a grant for *Ordinaries*, whether the directions of the Conference as to quarterly and annual accounts have been observed.

## IV. MINISTERIAL SUPPORT.

**272** One leading feature of the financial arrangements of the Methodist economy is, that Ministers receive *support* according to the requirements of themselves and their families, and not *salaries* according to the value which may be placed upon their services. Married Ministers are therefore provided for on a scale different from that of unmarried Ministers; and married Ministers with families on a scale different from married Ministers without families.

**273** The Conference rejoices in the efforts that have been made from time to time towards securing an improved scale of Ministerial Allowances, and thankfully acknowledges the liberality which has enabled so many Circuits to pay a stipend of £120 to married Ministers, and £40 to unmarried. While the Conference expresses the hope that this minimum may speedily be reached on all Circuits, yet, in order to prevent misapprehension, it thinks it needful to say that it cannot undertake to secure, by grants from any funds at its disposal, that this minimum shall be attained in any particular Circuit. In the case of Circuits where the stipend of £100 for the married Minister is all that is paid, the stipend of the unmarried Minister on such Circuits should not exceed £30.

**274** Every Minister who, having travelled twelve years, still remains unmarried, shall be provided for as a married Minister. If there be not a sufficiency of furnished houses to meet the case of all the married Ministers, then, so far as may be necessary, junior married Ministers shall be stationed in those places where already the cost of lodgings is incurred for an unmarried Minister, and, in addition, a grant of £40 from the Home Mission Fund shall be paid to each of them. If in any case it shall be found impracticable to carry out this Rule, and that a Junior Married Minister be appointed to a country Circuit where there is not sufficient provision for board and lodging, then a slight increase of the special allowance of £40 shall be made to the Minister so circumstanced.

N.B.—Junior Ministers becoming widowers without children, shall be provided for as Junior Married Ministers.

### V. MINISTERS' RESIDENCES.

**275** It is the duty of the Circuit Stewards to see that suitable residences are provided for the Married Ministers appointed to their Circuits, and that the residences are suitably furnished; and that both furniture and residences are kept in proper repair. If the residence be Trust property it is the duty of the Superintendent to make an annual report to the District Meeting of its condition as regards repair.

**276** A suitable book has been prepared by order of the Conference in which to enter and preserve an inventory of the furniture in each Minister's Residence, and it is directed that this book shall be accurately and regularly kept in every Circuit.

**277** As to the *Furniture of Ministers' Residences* the following Rules have been adopted by the Conference:—

1. In the absence of any special reference in our Deeds of Trust to the furniture provided for the residences of our Ministers (whether the residence be Trust property or otherwise), the Conference thinks it needful to declare that the Ministers having the use and occupation of such furniture, together with the Circuit Stewards for the time being, are to be regarded as trustees on behalf of the Circuit, and are expected and required to use all possible care and diligence for the preservation of such furniture in good condition, and for its requisite renewal from time to time.

2. Ministers occupying such furnished residences are to be regarded as occupying them subject to similiar rules with reference to the delivery of possession at the end of their term as would apply in the case of the renting of a furnished house from an ordinary landlord; that is to say, they are bound to deliver up the furniture to the Stewards of the Circuit in the same good order in which it was received, due allowance being made for ordinary wear and tear.

3. All damage occasioned to furniture, and all breakage or loss of glass, delf, or other articles, arising from the neglect or fault of servants or others in the Ministers' household, if not repaired and made good by the Minister occupying the residence at the time, shall be reported by his successor to the following District Meeting, and the amount requisite to repair and make good the damage or loss shall be required to be paid forthwith by the Minister in fault.

4. Every Minister entering upon the occupation of any furnished residence shall be regarded as having received the furniture in good order, and shall be accountable for it as in such condition, unless the list in the Furniture Book specifies otherwise, or unless he at once corrects any misdescription in that list and calls the attention of the Steward to his correction.

5. Any Minister failing to leave in the Furniture Book a full list and proper description of the articles in the house, and to get the signature of a Circuit or a Society Steward to the list, shall be held accountable for any want of good order in which the furniture may be found by his successor.

## CHAPTER II.

## HOME MISSION AND CONTINGENT FUND.

### I. ORIGIN AND DESIGN.

**278** This Fund was originated at an early period in the history of Methodism by the Rev. John Wesley. It was at first applied to the liquidation of debts on those Chapels which had been already built; to provide means for calling out an additional number of Travelling Preachers; to meet the deficiencies of those Preachers who were stationed in the poorer Circuits in England, Scotland, Wales, and Ireland; and to defray certain necessary law expenses. At first it was called the General Fund, but after the name had been changed several times, it was resolved by the Conference of 1867 that it should thenceforth be called the *Home Mission and Contingent Fund*.

Originally the income of the Fund was obtained chiefly, if not exclusively, by the Yearly Collection made in the several Classes at the March visitation. But, from time to time, as the organization of the Connexion developed, additional sources of supply were provided; and while the establishment of a General Building and Chapel Fund relieved this Fund of any claims for aid towards the liquidation of Chapel debts, the scope of its operations in other respects has been enlarged.

In addition to sustaining, either wholly or in part, General Missionaries, Ministers labouring on Mission Stations, and Ministers labouring for the benefit of Wesleyans in the Army, this Fund is employed to assist Circuits which could not, without such aid, support the Ministers appointed to them. This is one of the most important modes in which it contributes to the maintenance and extension of the work of God; for without the help thus afforded many Ministers must be withdrawn from the spheres of labour where their services are greatly needed. The Fund also affords aid to Circuits to meet certain "*Extraordinary*" expenses to which they may occasionally be liable and which they cannot defray wholly from their own resources. And, as the name of the Fund implies, various "*Contingent*" expenses arising from year to year in the carrying on and development of the work, which the Conference oversees and directs, are defrayed from this Fund.

## II. SOURCES OF INCOME.

**279** The Sources of Income to the Fund are as follow:— (1) The Yearly Collection in the Classes made as hereafter set forth; (2) Collections at Public Meetings, and weekly, monthly, or annual subscriptions collected by adult or Juvenile Collectors on the several Circuits and Mission Stations; (3) Special Donations from liberal friends in Ireland or elsewhere; (4) Grants in aid of the Fund from the Committee of the Wesleyan Methodist Missionary Society, the English Home Mission and Contingent Fund, and the Connexional Book Room; (5) the proceeds of investments of benefactions to the Fund given or bequeathed for that purpose; and (6) Legacies which may from time to time be received to be applied to the current income.

**280** The following regulations apply to some of the foregoing sources of Income:

1. The Conference directs that a suitable paper setting forth the nature and claims of the *Yearly Collection*, be prepared and printed and sent in sufficient numbers to the Superintendents of Circuits and Mission Stations in order to its being read in each Class by the Leader immediately previous to the quarterly visitation for the renewal of tickets of membership in December or March. And Superintendents are required, either themselves or by their Colleagues, afterwards to make application at the quarterly visitation to every Member in all the Classes in their respective Circuits for subscriptions towards this Collection.

2. Superintendents are directed to endeavour to form on every Circuit and Mission Station an ASSOCIATION, consisting of a *Committee* with a *Treasurer* and a *Secretary*, to promote the objects of the Fund; also to appoint *Juvenile* and *Adult Collectors*, and to return to the *General Secretary* of the Fund, for publication, a list of contributors of two shillings and sixpence, and upwards, per annum.

3. It is further directed that at each Financial District Meeting in August, arrangements shall be made for the holding of public meetings and the preaching of sermons on behalf of the Fund; and it is recommended that Lay gentlemen be appointed to accompany the Home Mission deputation for the Districts. Inquiry shall be made at the District Meetings in May respecting the efforts made on each Circuit and Station on behalf of the Fund.

4. The General Secretary of the Fund shall from time to time as may be expedient prepare and issue for general distribution a short paper explanatory of the nature, objects and necessities of the Fund.

### III. GENERAL RULES OF ADMINISTRATION.

**281** The Fund shall be administered under the direction of the "General Committee of Management," subject to such Rules as the Conference shall from time to time adopt. A Report of the proceedings of the Committee in relation to the Fund shall be presented annually to the Conference.

**282** Two Treasurers shall be appointed annually by the Conference, a Minister and a Layman. The Treasurers shall have an account opened in a Bank in their joint names, and all collections, contributions, grants and legacies remitted to them, or to either of them, on behalf of the Fund, shall be lodged to the credit of this account, and payments made thereout according to rule. The accounts shall be audited by Auditors nominated by the Committee and appointed by the Conference.

**283** For so long a period as may be found necessary, a Minister of competent experience and ability shall be set apart from ordinary Circuit work as the *General Secretary* of the Fund, to whom all communications on the business of the Fund (other than remittances to the Treasurers) shall be addressed.

**284** The *Grants* which from time to time may be made from the Fund, whether for *Ordinary* or for *Extraordinary* Expenditure, shall be set down as Grants to the Circuits, and not to individual Ministers. The Grants shall be paid, when due, to the Superintendent Minister, who shall account for them to the Circuit Stewards, or other persons entitled to receive them.

**285** Grants for "*Ordinary Expenditure*" shall be paid quarterly by the Treasurers; not later than the first week in October, January and March, for the first three quarters; and through the District Financial Secretaries at the Conference for the fourth quarter. Grants for "*Extraordinaries*" shall be paid when the conditions of the Grant are fulfilled, or as the Committee of Management shall direct.

**286** In order that the sums necessary for the payment of Grants may be in hands, the Conference peremptorily requires that the amount of subscriptions and collections for the Fund shall be remitted by Superintendents of Circuits, or by Circuit Treasurers, to the Treasurers of the Fund as soon as those amounts shall have been received.

**287** The "*Contingent Expenses*" which are defrayed by the Fund include expenses of Representatives deputed to attend other Conferences; expenses of Committee of Privileges, and other special Committees; official expenses of Chairmen and Secretaries of Districts; expenses of holding Minor District Meetings; travelling expenses of Ministers elected to attend Conference when those expenses are not chargeable to any other Fund, and are not borne by the Circuits; together with sundry other expenses incidental to the carrying out of the Connexional system.

It is directed that the official expenses of Chairmen and Secretaries of Districts, and any expenses incurred in connection with Minor District Meetings, shall be entered in the Minutes of the Annual District Meetings, and reported to the General Committee of Management in order to their being paid by the Treasurers of the Fund.

The Conference calls attention to the fact that some Circuits pay the expenses of their Ministers elected to attend Conference, and it urges the propriety and necessity of other Circuits following this example.

**288** It is directed that the expenses of the Home Mission Deputation to the several Districts shall be defrayed by the Treasurers of the Fund, instead of being made a charge upon the Circuits visited by the Deputation.

289. The Superintendent of each Circuit or Station receiving a Grant from the Fund for ordinary expenditure shall furnish once in three years, or when required, at the May District Meeting, a report of the moral and religious condition of the sphere of labour included in his Circuit. Such reports shall be forwarded immediately afterwards to the General Secretary in order to the preparation of the Annual Report.

### IV. RULES RELATING TO GRANTS TOWARDS "ORDINARY EXPENDITURE."

290 The Annual District Meetings are directed to examine into the necessities of the several Circuits and Mission Stations applying for Grants from the Fund towards "*Ordinary Expenditure,*" and to recommend to the General Committee of Management the amount of Grant which, in their judgment, is likely to be needful in each case for the coming year. The Committee shall consider, at its Meeting in May, all such applications, and the judgment of the District Meetings thereon, and shall report to the Conference its own recommendations concerning them. A list of the Grants as approved by the Conference shall be published in the Minutes of the Conference, as well as in the Report of the Fund, and shall be final for the year; except in such cases as may be reserved by the Conference for further consideration by the Committee of Management.

291 The General Committee of Management, in determining the amount of Grant which may be needful in each case, shall have due regard to the recommendations of the Conference as to the Minimum of Ministers' Stipend (see par. 273) with a view to promote the attainment of that minimum as speedily and as extensively as possible.

**292** All applications for Grants shall be made on the "Form" provided for the purpose, and shall set forth in detail the amount of the Income and Expenditure of the Circuit or Station making the application, with the amount of Grant required, and the conditions, if any, as to the amount to be paid for Ministers' Stipend. Forms of application will be supplied by the General Secretary of the Fund.

**293** Grants towards "Ordinary Expenditure" are not to be considered, or applied, as Grants towards Ministers' Stipend only, but as Grants towards the whole of the expenditure set forth in the "Form of Application."

**294** Superintendents of Circuits and Mission Stations receiving Grants towards "Ordinary Expenditure" are required as soon as possible after the 31st December (and not later than the month of February following) to send to the General Secretary of the Fund a statement of the Circuit Income and Expenditure for the year. (See pars. 270, 271 for Rules relating to Circuit Accounts.)

### V. RULES RELATING TO GRANTS TOWARDS "EXTRAORDINARY EXPENDITURE."

**295** Grants towards (1) expenses incurred by *Affliction* in Ministers' families; (2) the cost of *Supply* rendered necessary by the death, affliction, or necessary absence of a Minister; (3) the cost of providing *Furniture* for additional Married Ministers' Residences, or newly erected or purchased Ministers' Residences; and (4) Grants towards *Furnishing* or *Repairing* Ministers' Residences on feeble dependent Circuits and Mission Stations are accounted *Grants for Extraordinaries*, and may be made by the General Committee of Management subject to the following Rules:—

1. All applications for Grants of this class must have the

sanction of the Quarterly Meeting of the Circuit or Station concerned, and must be recommended by a District Meeting before being considered by the General Committee of Management.

N.B. Applications for Grants for *Furniture* or *Repairs* may be recommended by either the *Financial* or the *Annual* District Meeting. They must be made on the Form provided for the purpose, which may be obtained from the General Secretary of the Fund.

2. The Conference expects that before presenting any application for a Grant towards expenses incurred by *Affliction* in the families of their Ministers, or for *Supply* rendered necessary by such affliction, or otherwise, the Circuits making the applications will have done their utmost to meet these expenses.

N.B. Grants for Supply cannot be made in the case of the failure in health of Preachers on Trial. (See pars. 78, 79 for Rules concerning Supplies.)

3. The Conference will determine, from year to year, the total sum which may be allocated by the Committee of Management in Grants for *Affliction*, and Grants to feeble Dependent Circuits and Mission Stations for *Renewal of Furniture* and for *Repairs of Residences*; and the Committee is required not to go beyond the sum specified.

4. In all cases of application for Grants on account of *Affliction* the Minister with whom, or in whose family, the affliction has occurred is directed to communicate to the General Secretary of the Fund such information as to the facts of the case as may be necessary.

5. Grants for *Furniture*, not exceeding £40 in each case, may be made to Non-Dependent Circuits, as well as to Dependent Circuits, to assist in furnishing Residences for

*Additional Married Ministers*, provided that no such grant be paid unless the Residence is substantially furnished as certified after personal inspection by the Chairman of the District, or by some Minister deputed by him, and by a Circuit Steward appointed by the District Meeting, such Steward not being of the Circuit in which the expenditure is made. Grants may also be made of such amount as the Committee of Management may judge necessary, to assist in providing additional furniture for *newly erected* or *purchased* Ministers' Residences which are not Residences for "Additional Married Ministers."

Forms of Certificate may be obtained from the General Secretary.

6. Grants for *Renewal of Furniture* and for *Repairs of Ministers' Residences* shall be confined entirely to feeble Dependent Circuits and Mission Stations. In the consideration of applications for such Grants the General Committee of Management shall give precedence to applications for Grants for *Repairs*, inasmuch as these may sometimes be urgently needed for the purpose of preserving Trust property from further injury and decay.

7. Grants for Repairs of Ministers' Residences are not to be made unless the sanction of the General Committee of Management, or of the Sub-Committee, has been obtained previous to the expenditure being made; and Grants for Furniture or Repairs are not to be paid by the Treasurers until the Superintendents of the Circuits concerned have certified to the General Secretary, on the Form provided, that the conditions are fulfilled. Grants not claimed within a year are to be considered as lapsed Grants, unless notice is given to the Officers of the Fund that the Circuits will be in a condition to claim the Grants in the course of the following year.

## VI. RULES RELATING TO REVISION OF CIRCUITS AND THE APPOINTMENT OF ADDITIONAL MINISTERS.

**296** All recommendations affecting the *Revision* of Circuits and Missions, and all applications for *Additional Ministers* which may be approved by the District Meetings shall be forwarded to the General Secretary of the Fund for consideration by the General Committee of Management.

**297** No Circuit or Mission Station is to be divided without the consent of the Quarterly Meeting; but the District Meeting may recommend an alteration in the boundaries of a Circuit or Mission Station. In every case in which a division is recommended, the record should state clearly the proposed boundary lines, especially in towns; and the number of Members and of preaching places belonging to each division.

**298** When any changes have been made in the boundaries of a Circuit or Mission Station by the transfer of Members and preaching places to another Circuit or Station, the Superintendent shall furnish lists of Members and preaching places to the Superintendent to whose care the same have been transferred, together with all other particulars of information which may be necessary.

**299** No application for an *additional Minister* to be engaged in the regular work can be entertained unless a plan stating distinctly how and where he is to be employed and how provided for, be produced in writing in conjunction with the application.

**300** If an *additional Minister* be appointed to any Circuit or Station, and if the appointment so made be that of an *unmarried Minister*, or of a *Preacher on Trial*, the Fund shall be charged with, at least, £60 a year, in addition to any grant to the Circuit on account of the appointment; and this extra charge shall be carried to the credit of a Reserve Fund, to assist in providing a furnished residence for a Married Minister at the end of five years.

### VII. RULES RELATING TO THE GENERAL MISSION.

**301** The Home Mission Fund is available for the support of Missionaries who are not attached to any definite Circuit or Station, but who labour as occasion may serve in all parts of the kingdom, either in established Congregations in conjunction with the stationed Ministers, or in Special out-door or Tent Services, to assist in promoting a revival of God's work. The following are the rules which have been adopted with reference to the appointment and the work of the General Missionaries:—

1. Not more than two General Missionaries shall be appointed from year to year; and this number shall be maintained, if possible, for the future.

2. The General Committee of Management is authorized to provide and furnish a house in Dublin as a residence for one of the General Missionaries, and a house in Belfast as a residence for the other.

3. The appointment of any Minister to the General Mission, like all other appointments, is liable to change from year to year; and no one shall be continued in this special work longer than six years, at the utmost.

4. The General Committee of Management is authorized, at any time when it becomes necessary or desirable to make a new appointment, to enter into correspondence with such Minister as may seem specially fitted for the work, with the view of obtaining his consent to nominate him, through the Stationing Committee, to the Conference for an appointment as General Missionary.

5. The Superintendents of Circuits are directed to send their suggestions in reference to the employment of the General Missionaries to the General Secretary of the Home Mission Fund; and the General Secretary, with the Sub-Committee of Management, is authorized to prepare a plan for the visitation of the different Circuits of the Connexion by the Missionaries during the year.

6. In order to assist in meeting the expenditure, Circuits asking for the services of the General Missionaries are requested to make a special collection during the mission in aid of the Fund.

### VIII. RULES RELATING TO WORK IN THE ARMY AND ROYAL NAVY.

**302** A Committee shall be appointed annually by the Conference, which shall have the oversight of all matters connected with the carrying on of our work in the Army and Navy; this Committee shall be denominated the Army and Navy Committee, and shall consist of the Treasurers and the Secretary of the Home Mission and Contingent Fund, the Minister appointed as Chaplain at the Curragh Camp, with three Ministers and five Laymen resident in the Dublin District, and four Ministers and four Laymen resident in other Districts.

**303** All correspondence with the War office and Admiralty, except on matters of routine, shall be conducted through the Secretary of the Committee; and the Committee shall have authority from time to time, to issue circulars of information for the instruction of Army and Navy Ministers.

N.B.—The minutes of proceedings of the Committee shall be reported to the General Committee of Management at its Meeting in May.

**304** Ministers stationed where there are Garrisons and Naval Ports, are instructed to make such arrangements with the Naval and Military authorities as may be necessary for the benefit of Wesleyan Soldiers and Seamen, in concert with the Army and Navy Committee. In Garrison towns where there is more than one Chapel which Soldiers can conveniently attend, the Committee, after consulting with the Ministers concerned, shall direct to which of the Chapels the Troops shall be marched, and no change in this arrangement shall be made without the authority of the Committee. Ministers stationed in towns which are not regular stations for Troops, but where detachments of Troops may from time to time be quartered, are required to communicate to the Secretary of the Committee information of the arrival of such detachments and of the number of Wesleyans therein.

**305** In all stations where Ministers are appointed to officiate to Wesleyan Troops, quarterly reports and returns shall be forwarded to the Secretary of the Committee on "Forms" which shall be provided for the purpose; and the Chairmen of Districts shall call the attention of Superintendents at the Financial District Meeting to this rule.

**306** As it is of the highest importance in order to ascertain correctly the strength of Methodism in the Army that all returns should be made at the same time, the Conference directs that all Superintendents of Circuits or Stations from which there are any Military or Naval returns to be forwarded, shall in future make the annual returns required at the same date as the returns from British Stations viz:—December 31st. If a return of women and children be considered necessary, this return shall be made at the same time but in a separate column.

N.B.—The Secretary of the Committee shall provide and supply the necessary "Forms" for these returns, which shall be similar to those in use by the British Conference.

**307** The following regulations respecting allocation of the capitation allowances, now paid by her Majesty's Government for Wesleyan Troops, have been adopted by the Conference:—

1. In Circuits or Stations which do not receive any grant from the Home Mission and Contingent Fund, for the support of the Minister who takes the pastoral oversight of the Troops, one half of the capitation allowance shall be paid to the Minister discharging such duties, and the other half to the Circuit Stewards.

2. In Circuits or Stations receiving grants from the Home Mission and Contingent Fund, except in cases where special arrangements are made, the capitation allowance shall be apportioned as follows:—

(1.) If the amount do not exceed £1 5s. per quarter, the whole of the allowance shall be paid to the Minister who discharges the duties.

(2.) If the amount exceed £1 5s. per quarter, the surplus shall be equally divided between the Minister and the Home Mission and Contingent Fund.

(3.) Aid-giving Circuits shall be dealt with on the same principle as non-dependent Circuits.

### IX. MISCELLANEOUS REGULATIONS.

**308** *Removal Expenses.* For the purpose of securing uniformity as to the payment of the Removal Expenses of Ministers on all classes of Circuits dependent on the Home Mission Fund, it is directed that when those expenses shall have been ascertained and certified by the Financial District

Meeting and approved by the General Committee of Management, they shall be paid by the Treasurers of the Fund; and the means of making such payments shall be provided by deducting each year from the first quarterly instalment of the *Grant for Ordinaries*, the sum of £2 for each Minister stationed in those Circuits.

**309** *Allowance for Furniture to Ministers becoming Supernumerary, and to Widows of Ministers.* Every Minister when he becomes permanently a Supernumerary, and every Widow of a Minister who has died before becoming a Supernumerary, is entitled to an allowance of £40 towards furnishing a residence. This allowance was formerly paid by the Treasurers of the English Home Mission Fund, but in consideration of the annual Grant from that Fund for the work in Ireland having been increased from £650 to £800 a year, the allowance shall henceforth be met by the Home Mission and Contingent Fund for Ireland, and the Treasurers are accordingly authorized to make the payments.

**310** *Payment to Board of Public Works of Instalments on Loans for Ministers' Residences.* Whereas it has been considered expedient that the provisions of the "Glebes Loans Act" should be made available, as far as possible, to assist in the erection or purchase of Ministers' Residences, and whereas many such loans have been obtained, it is directed that in the case of dependent Circuits and Mission Stations, and in such other cases as the Conference may determine, the half-yearly instalments, as they become due, shall be paid by the Treasurers of the Fund and entered in their Annual Statement of Accounts. Circuits receiving *Grants for Ordinaries* shall have their Grants diminished in proportion.

**311** *Donations on Annuity.* When any money shall be absolutely paid to the Treasurers of the Home Mission Fund as such, in consideration of any annuity or annuities to be paid by the said Treasurers, the funds, property and income belonging to the Fund shall be charged with and be liable to pay such annuity or annuities ; and a declaration to that effect, signed by the General Treasurers and the Secretary or the Secretaries for the time being of the Fund, shall be delivered to the party or parties who shall be entitled to such annuity or annuities ; and a competent sum (to be determined by the General Committee of Management, according to the circumstances of each particular case) shall thereupon be so invested as to make adequate provision for the due payment of such annuity or annuities, so long as the same shall continue, and until all payments to be made in respect thereof shall be fully discharged and satisfied.

## CHAPTER III.

## FUNDS FOR MINISTERS' CHILDREN.

### I. THE CHILDREN'S FUND.

**312** In 1822 the Conference resolved that the usual allowances for the *Maintenance* of Ministers' Children should be chargeable upon the Circuits "according to the principle of proportion of numbers in Society;" this was the beginning of the plan which issued in the formation of the "Children's Fund." The allowance for *Education* was not at first embraced in the plan of *assessment in proportion to number of members* but was provided on a somewhat different principle; a few years afterwards both classes of "Allowance" were included in the "Assessment."

In 1860 the basis of "Assessment" was changed from a "rate per Member" to "a rate per Minister according to the number of Ministers in the respective Circuits;" in the same year the children of Supernumerary and deceased Ministers were admitted to the benefit of the usual allowance for Maintenance in addition to the allowance for Education to which they had been previously entitled. In 1862 the organization of the Children's Fund was completed by the appointment of a Treasurer and a Secretary distinct from the Treasurers and Secretary of the Home Mission and Contingent Fund, who had previously been charged with carrying out the arrangements concerning Ministers' Children.

## THE CHILDREN'S FUND.

313 The following are the Rules and regulations relating to the Children's Fund:—

1. The Conference shall annually appoint a Minister and a Layman as Treasurers of the Fund, and a Minister as Secretary. It is the duty of the Secretary to keep a correct register of children who are claimants on the Fund, and to report from year to year to the General Committee of Management the number of new claimants, the number who have ceased to be claimants, the total number of claimants for the year, and any other matter of interest in relation to the Fund. The accounts of the Treasurers shall be annually audited by Auditors nominated by the General Committee of Management, and shall be published in the Report of the Home Mission and Contingent Fund.

2 *The object of the Fund* is to provide allowances for the maintenance and education of the children of Ministers in connexion with the Irish Methodist Conference, in such manner as shall be most equitable, and least burdensome, to the several Circuits and Stations.

3. *The Income of the Fund* is provided by an annual "Assessment" on each Circuit, Station, Institution or Department, to which Ministers in full work, or Preachers on Trial, are appointed, in proportion to the number appointed to each. The rate of assessment is, at present, £25 per Minister, per annum, but the rate may be varied from time to time, as the Conference may direct.

4. *Claimants on the Fund* include children of Ministers in active work, and of Supernumerary and deceased Ministers. The allowances are £5 10s. per annum for maintenance until sixteen years of age, and £10 additional for education from eight to sixteen years of age. Children of Ministers who retire from our work, or who from any cause, cease to be

recognised as in connexion with the Methodist Conference in Ireland, have no claim upon the Fund.

5. For children who have been born and have died during the year, one year's maintenance shall be included in the accounts of the following year.

6. The year shall commence on the 1st of July. Claims shall cease for all children who shall have died before that date, and for those born after it no claim shall be entered until the next Conference.

7. Ministers who shall marry after having become permanent Supernumeraries, shall not have any claim for the children of such marriages.

8. The allowances from the Fund become due at the end of September, December, March and June, and are payable not later than the fifteenth of the following month for the first three quarters, and at the Conference, through the District Financial Secretaries, for the June quarter.

9. Circuit Stewards are required to account quarterly with the Superintendents of Circuits for the amount of the "Assessment" on the Circuit, and the Superintendents shall account with the Treasurers of the Fund.

10. The payment of allowances for Children of Supernumerary or deceased Ministers shall be made through the Superintendents of the Circuits on which they reside.

## II. THE MINISTERS' SONS' FUND.

314 In addition to the "Allowances" for Education provided by the Children's Fund, special provision is made for the Education of Ministers' Sons by means of a Supplementary Fund called the *Ministers' Sons' Fund*. Certain sums of money having been allocated by the Committee of the "Fund for the Increase of Wesleyan Agency in Ireland," and by the

Committee of Testamentary Bequests, for the education of the Sons of the Ministers it was resolved that the said sums should be invested in the names of ten Trustees (five ministers and five laymen) appointed by the Conference, and that the principal should remain untouched; the annually accruing interest and that only, being available to supplement the ordinary Connexional Allowances for education.

315 The following are the Regulations affecting the Administration of the Fund:—

1. The annual proceeds of the Fund thus created shall not be distributed in grants to individual parents, but shall be applied for the education of the sons of our Ministers in connection with that of the sons of our people in a Methodist educational establishment.

2. Admission into such an Institution shall be granted, if the income of the Fund will allow, to all sons of Ministers of the age of ten; residence not to continue longer than the age of sixteen. If applications be more numerous than vacancies, the claims of those parents who have had no son educated on the Foundation shall have preference over the claims of those who have had one or more so educated for three years or upwards. If there still be an excess of applications, precedence shall be decided by the standing of the fathers in the Ministry; and in case the standing of the fathers be equal, the son of a deceased father shall have preference over the son of a living one. If both fathers are living or both deceased, precedence shall be given to the senior boy, or as the Committee of selection may decide.

An additional year may be given to any of the boys on the Foundation provided there be funds for the purpose, and that no boy who would be entitled to claim admission is thereby excluded.

3. The parents of boys selected by the Committee shall be at liberty to choose between Wesley College in Dublin and the Methodist College in Belfast as their place of education.

4. The sum to be allowed from the Children's Fund on behalf of the boys so elected, shall be determined by the Conference from time to time as may be necessary; the sum to be paid for their board and education shall be matter of arrangement between the Trustees of the Ministers' Sons' Fund and the Institutions; and such payment shall be made by the Trustees as may be necessary to make up the balance.

5. The Treasurers and the Secretary of the Children's Fund together with the Treasurers and the Secretary of the Trustees of the Ministers' Sons' Fund, shall be a Committee for the selection of boys who may from time to time be eligible for admission to Wesley College, Dublin, or the Methodist College, Belfast, on the Foundation of the Fund, and for the carrying out of all regulations which may be made affecting such admissions.

The Secretary of the Children's Fund shall be the Secretary of this Committee, and to him all communications relating to the admission of boys to, or their withdrawal from, the Colleges shall be addressed.

6. The ordinary rules of the Colleges with reference to the notice required previous to the withdrawal of a pupil, shall be regarded as applying to all Ministers' Sons on the Foundation, except such as are withdrawn on the completion of their term. For boys withdrawn in the course of the year, after due notice to the Secretary of the Fund, the usual allowance from the Children's Fund, shall be paid to the parent for the remaining quarters of the year.

7. The Governor of Wesley College and the President of the Methodist College shall, each year, be informed by the

Secretary of the Committee immediately after the Conference, and again immediately after Christmas, how many boys are placed on the Foundation for the respective Colleges for the next half year; and the Treasurers of these Institutions shall be entitled to receive the stipulated allowances for that number for the two quarters following, provided that, if from an insufficiency of applicants, or, of boys eligible to be received on the Foundation, the Committee find it impossible to fill up vacancies which may occur in the course of the half year, they shall be entitled to send a boy for each such vacancy in the following quarter without charge.

8. The payment to the Colleges on account of boys on the Foundation shall be made by the Treasurers of the Children's Fund, and in order to this the Trustees of the Ministers' Sons' Fund shall, through their Treasurer, pay to the Treasurers of the Children's Fund, in the course of each year so much of the proceeds of their investments as on their report of the state of their funds the Conference may have directed.

9. The amount annually appropriated from the Ministers' Sons' Fund for boys on the Foundation shall be set forth each year in the published statement of Income and Expenditure of the Children's Fund.

### III. THE MINISTERS' DAUGHTERS' FUND.

**316** By means of appropriations from the "Thanksgiving Fund" and the "Jubilee Fund" and through the benefactions of the late Sir William M'Arthur, K.C.M.G., special provision is made for the Education of Ministers' Daughters, in addition to the "Allowances" for that purpose from the Children's Fund. The sums constituting the Endowment for Ministers' Daughters are held in trust by the Governors of the Methodist College, Belfast.

317 The Regulations affecting the administration of the Fund are the following:—

1. The annual proceeds of the Fund shall not be distributed in grants to individual parents, but shall be applied for education in the Methodist College, Belfast.

2. Admission shall be granted to the daughters of Ministers at the age of twelve; residence not to continue longer than the age of sixteen. If applications be more numerous than vacancies the claims of those parents who have derived no advantage from either the Ministers' Sons' Fund or the Ministers' Daughters' Fund shall have preference over the claims of those who have received such advantages. If there should still be an excess of applications, precedence shall be decided by the rules which apply to similar cases in the Ministers' Sons' Fund. (See par. 315).

3. The full allowance from the Children's Fund for both Maintenance and Education shall be paid to the Treasurer of the College for each girl on the Foundation.

4. The ordinary rules of the College with reference to the notice required previous to the withdrawal of a pupil shall apply to all Ministers' Daughters on the Foundation except such as are withdrawn on the completion of their term.

5. Should any parent withdraw a daughter before the full term of residence is completed, he shall not thereby acquire the right to have another daughter on the Foundation for the remainder of the term.

6. The Governors of the College shall annually report to the Conference how many daughters of Ministers can be taken on the Foundation.

7. The President of the College, the Vice-President and the Secretary of the Conference, the Secretary of the Board

of Governors, with the Officers of the Children's Fund shall be a Committee of selection to meet during the Conference; the Secretary of the Children's Fund shall be the Convener of the Committee.

# CHAPTER IV.

## SUPERNUMERARY METHODIST MINISTERS' AND MINISTERS' WIDOWS' FUND.

### I. ORIGIN.

**318** This Fund had its origin in the Centenary movement of 1839. Previously to this there was no distinct and regular provision made by the Methodist Societies for the support of Supernumerary Ministers and the Widows of deceased Ministers. There was the "Legalized Fund," or, as it is now designated, "The Itinerant Methodist Preachers' Annuitant Society;" but this was a Fund created and supported mainly by the subscriptions of the Preachers themselves, and of the nature of a *Mutual Benefit Society.* There was also a Fund termed "The Methodist Preachers' Auxiliary Fund," which was sustained by the subscriptions of the Methodist people, but this was of the nature of a *Merciful Fund*, which only met cases of necessity, or peculiar difficulty, by *grants in aid;* it did not embrace all Supernumerary Ministers and Ministers' Widows, and did not provide a permanent annuity for any.

The generous laymen who took a leading part in the Centenary movement urged that arrangements should be made for a more regular and adequate provision for the Ministers who were "worn out" in the service of the Methodist Church, and for the Widows of such as had died; a plan was prepared for this purpose, and in the year 1840 the proposed Fund was organized.

The Supernumerary Ministers and Ministers' Widows of the Irish Conference were at first embraced in the plan for the organization and administration of the Fund, and this arrangement continued for many years. But it was eventually judged expedient that a separate Fund should be established for Ireland; and, in order to this, it was agreed by the English Conference of 1872 that £20,000 of the capital then standing to the credit of the Fund should be paid to Trustees to be appointed by the Irish Conference, who should "maintain this sum in its integrity" as a "nucleus of a Fund" for the Supernumerary Ministers and Widows connected with the Irish Conference. This arrangement was carried out during the following year: and the invested capital thus acquired was considerably increased as the result of a movement set on foot at the Irish Conference of 1874. The capital of the Fund was further increased in 1878 as one of the "Terms of Union" between "the two principal Methodist bodies in Ireland" then happily effected.

## II. DESIGNATION.

319 The Fund shall be called the Supernumerary Methodist Ministers' and Ministers' Widows' (Ireland) Fund.

## III. OBJECT.

320 The object of the Fund is to make some provision for Ministers connected with the Methodist Conference in Ireland, who, on account of age or infirmity, or for any cause which the Conference may deem sufficient, shall be declared Supernumerary; and for the Widows of Ministers who may have died in connexion with the Conference.

## IV. INCOME.

321 The Income of the Fund shall be derived from the following sources, viz:—(1.) Annual Subscriptions and

Congregational Collections, Donations, Legacies, &c., in the several Circuits. (2.) A sum of £3 each for every Minister, and Preacher on Trial, in Circuit work, to be included in the "Assessment" on the Circuits, and a like sum for every Minister or Preacher on Trial in other service than Circuit work to be included in the "Assessment" on the Institutions or Departments in which they may be engaged; such Assessments shall be paid with the "Assessment" for the Children's Fund, and shall be accounted for by the Treasurers of that Fund. (3) The Interest and Dividends arising from the Invested Capital, which shall be paid to the Treasurers half-yearly by the Trustees.

Collecting Books shall be circulated in all our Circuits, and suitable Collectors appointed to obtain subscriptions; and, where practicable, a Committee shall be appointed in each Circuit to co-operate with the Ministers in promoting the interests of this Fund. A public collection shall be taken up annually in our several Chapels on behalf of the Fund.

### V. RULES OF ADMINISTRATION.

322 The following are the Rules regulating the Administration of the Fund:—

The Scale of Allowances shall be as follows, viz:—

1. The number of years of Ministerial travelling shall be the basis of calculation.

Supernumerary Ministers shall receive a minimum allowance of £14 with £1 additional for each year of travelling.

Ministers' Widows shall receive a minimum allowance of £14, with 10s. additional for each year of their husband's travelling; except in case of disparity of age, as hereinafter provided.

2. When a Minister's Widow is not more than *ten* years

younger than her deceased husband, the full allowance, in accordance with the "Scale of Allowances" existing at the time, shall be paid. If she be more than *ten* years younger, *one-tenth* of the full allowance shall be deducted for each year, or part of a year, over *ten*. No allowance shall be paid if the disparity be *twenty* years.

3. With reference to claimants on the Fund in 1882 when the above rule was made, and with reference to Ministers' wives then living who become claimants, this rule shall not take effect so as to *lessen* the allowance they would have had under the former rule; but it shall take effect in all cases in which it *increases* the former allowances.

All marriages taking place after the passing of this rule, whether they be first or second marriages, shall come under its operation.

N.B.—The following is the "former rule" referred to in the preceding paragraph: "Ministers' Widows who are *twenty* years younger than their deceased husbands, shall have no claim on the Fund; and those who are *twelve* years younger, shall have a claim only for *one half* of the ordinary allowance."

4. The amounts to which the claimants are severally entitled shall be payable half-yearly in advance, on the first day of July and the first day of January, respectively; and they shall be remitted by the Treasurers as soon afterward as possible.

5. Any Minister declared by the Conference to be a Supernumerary for other cause than ill-health, and having travelled not more than *eighteen* years, shall be entitled to receive the aid of this Fund for the term of two years; or, if he decides on engaging in business, a sum equal to two years' allowances. If he shall not so decide, his case shall be specially considered by the Conference at the expiration of

the period of two years; and, unless the Conference should then direct otherwise, he shall have no further claim upon the Fund.

6. In the case of any Supernumerary who has travelled *eighteen* years or longer, and who is able to go into business, or of any Widow claimant who actually enters into business, the officers are authorized and required, for the mutual benefit of both parties, to endeavour to make arrangements for the relinquishment of all future claims on the part of such Supernumerary or Widow by the payment of one sum. (See par. 116 for rule concerning Supernumeraries who enter into business,)

7. No woman marrying a Supernumerary after he has been declared such by the Conference, shall, after his decease, have any claim upon the Fund, unless she had been previously receiving from it as a Widow, in which case her original claim shall revive.

8. If a Widow claimant marry she shall forfeit all claim upon the Fund ; unless she marries a Minister in connexion with the Methodist Conference in Ireland; in which case, should she survive him, her original claim shall revive, or shall merge in the claim, if higher, of her second widowhood; regard being had in all cases to the rule as to disparity of years.

9. Any Supernumerary removing from Ireland to reside elsewhere must have the special permission of the Conference for such removal to entitle him to receive any payment from the Fund. When claimants reside out of Ireland, a certificate shall be required from the Superintendent of the Circuit in which they reside, that they are alive, and members of the Methodist Society at the date on which each payment becomes due.

10. If any Supernumerary or Widow shall cease to be a member of the Methodist Society, he or she shall cease to have any claim upon the Fund.

11. When through death or otherwise any Supernumerary or Widow shall cease to be a claimant on the Fund, the Superintendent of the Circuit in which he or she lived shall forthwith inform the Treasurers, and shall also transmit the name and address of any Widow to be entered on the Register, with any change of residence which may take place in the case of Supernumeraries or Widows.

12. On the death of a claimant the sum of five pounds shall be paid towards funeral expenses. Should the Officers of the Fund consider that a pressing necessity exists, this amount may be augmented; the sum granted, however, in no case to exceed ten pounds.

# CHAPTER V.
# THE CHAPEL FUND AND TRUST AFFAIRS.

### I. ORIGIN OF THE FUND.

**323** In 1820 the Conference cordially approved and affectionately recommended to the Methodist people a plan for the "establishment of a Fund for liquidating debts on Chapels and Preachers' dwellings, and to assist in the erection of new ones." The "plan" proposed a collection in every Class of one penny per month from every member, and a like sum, or whatever they might choose above that, from "friends who were not in Society" who might be willing to assist. A Treasurer was to be appointed in every Circuit, and a proper person appointed in every Class to receive and pay over the monthly subscriptions.

The Fund was designated the "Building and Chapel Fund," and a Committee was appointed, partly chosen by the Conference, and partly elected by the District Meetings, for the management of the Fund. In 1865 the Conference resolved that the Committee should be called the "Building and Chapel Committee," and that its duties should include, in addition to the administration of the Chapel Fund, a general oversight of the Trust Property of the Connexion. Various regulations have been adopted since, which are set forth in this chapter. The Fund does not now afford aid for the erection or repairs of Ministers' Residences.

## II. GENERAL RULES.

**324** The Chapel Fund is administered under the direction of the General Committee of Management. The Conference annually appoints two Treasurers of the Fund, a Minister and a Layman; a Secretary; and a Registrar of Deeds. The Treasurers shall keep the accounts of the Fund in some convenient Bank, in their joint names, and shall submit them annually to Auditors nominated by the General Committee of Management and appointed by the Conference.

**325** The Registrar has charge of all Deeds and documents relating to Trust Property which are lodged in the Conference Safe. It is his duty to make and keep a list of such documents as are committed to his care; to keep the General Register, which contains a brief quotation from each Deed reciting Trustees, terms of holding, &c, written up to date; to correspond with the District Chapel Secretaries (appointed as hereafter specified) when necessary, in order that their Registers may exactly agree with his; and to report to the General Committee of Management, at its annual Meeting in May, as to the documents received for lodgment in the "Safe," and the changes, if any, in the documents formerly lodged.

**326** The Income of the Fund is derived from (1) Public Collections, in the Chapels; (2) Subscriptions in the Classes according to the Original rule; (3) Subscriptions from Chapel Trust Funds; and (4) Donations and Legacies.

The public collections for the Fund are to be made in the month of August or September and immediately remitted to the Treasurers.

The amount of Collections and Subscriptions on each Circuit shall be reported by the Superintendent at each Annual District Meeting, and if any considerable deficiency shall appear, the Chairman of the District shall make strict inquiry into the cause.

327 The annual income of the Fund shall, after defraying expenses, be applied by the General Committee of Management (subject to revision by the Conference) in grants towards the relief of Chapel debts, and in grants in aid of the erection of new Chapels.

328 Certain legacies and donations having by direction of the Conference been appropriated to the formation of a separate department of the Fund for the purpose of relieving embarrassed Chapel Trusts by Loans without interest, the General Committee of Management is empowered, as far as the Fund will permit, to make such loans subject to the conditions hereafter specified.

329 All applications for Grants, or Loans; for leave to build, enlarge, purchase, or repair; and all Schedules of Trust Property which have been submitted to the Annual District Meetings shall be forwarded without delay to the Secretary of the Chapel Fund, from whom the necessary Schedules and "Forms of Application" may previously be obtained.

330 The amount of debt reported upon Trust Property must embrace, as a separate item, the amount, if any, borrowed from the Board of Public Works under the provisions of the "Glebes Loans Act." (See section on Quarterly Meetings, par. 232.)

### III. RULES RELATING TO GRANTS AND LOANS.

331 The following are the rules to be observed by applicants for Grants or Loans for the relief of Chapel Trusts from debts, and to be regarded by the General Committee of Management in dealing with such applications:—

## 1. *Relief by Grants.*

1. All applications for grants must be submitted to the Annual District Meetings upon authorized Schedules.

2. No grant shall be paid on account of any Chapel that is not insured against fire, and that is not legally secured to the Connexion.

3. In no case shall the grant for any one Chapel exceed £200; and even in such case of grant, the amount shall be payable in two instalments; not more than £100 being paid in one year.

4. No application for relief shall be recommended by the District Meetings for any Chapel, unless the Trustees make an annual collection in aid of the Chapel Fund.

5. The Conference directs that the Secretary of the Chapel department shall transmit to the Chairman of each District an account of all cases of conditional grants made to Trusts within his District, in order that he may inquire at the Annual District Meeting whether the conditions have been fulfilled.

6. In all cases of conditional grants, the Treasurers shall, previous to payment, satisfy themselves that the conditions have been complied with.

7. If any additional outlay beyond the original contract for any building be incurred without the explicit sanction of the General Committee of Management, or its Sub-Committee, previously obtained in writing, in no such case shall any claim on the Chapel Fund be admitted.

8. In all cases in which applications for Grants are held over, Superintendents of Circuits are instructed to renew such applications through the Annual District Meeting.

9. In order to meet the case of feeble Circuits, where an unlooked for and urgent necessity arises for outlay in the repair of Chapels, and sufficient local funds cannot be obtained

for the purpose, the Sub-Committee of Management is empowered to make small grants from the Chapel Fund to assist in meeting such expenditure.

### 2. *Relief by Loans without Interest.*

1. Applications for loans must be made on the usual authorized "Form," and submitted to the Annual District Meeting for approval.

2. All loans must be repaid by half-yearly instalments; the period of repayment never to exceed ten years.

3. In each case of loan, satisfactory security for repayment shall be given, and also for the fulfilment of other conditions; the guarantee shall be made on a "Form" to be provided for that purpose, signed by such parties as the Committee may deem suitable.

4. Applicants shall produce their Trust deeds if required by the Committee.

### IV. ERECTIONS, ENLARGEMENTS, PURCHASES, &c.

332 Every application for permission to erect, enlarge, improve or purchase a Chapel, or to introduce an organ into a Chapel, must be with the consent of the Quarterly Meeting of the Circuit, and be presented to the District Meeting on a proper Schedule, signed by the Superintendent and by one or more of the acting or proposed Trustees. The approbation of the District Meeting, testified by the Chairman's signature, must be obtained before any such case can be sanctioned by the General Committee of Management.

333 In any case of urgency relating to the erection, enlargement, purchase, or sale of a Chapel, where it would be seriously detrimental to defer the consideration of the case till the time of the Financial or the Annual District Meeting, the

Chapel Sub-Committee of the District may consider such case, and on receiving from that Sub-Committee a Schedule properly filled up and signed, the General Committee of Management, or its Sub-Committee, is authorized to deal with the case as though it had passed the District Meeting. Any expense incurred by such meeting of the District Chapel Sub-Committee shall be borne by the Circuit or Mission making the application.

**334** The obligation to obtain the sanction of the General Committee of Management extends to all cases of erection, purchase, and enlargement; and to all cases of alteration and improvement, when any debt is incurred. The Committee shall be satisfied before giving their sanction to any case, either that the entire outlay shall be met, or that at least two-thirds of the amount of outlay shall have been subscribed.

The Committee shall also be satisfied that all land required is, or shall be, legally secured for the intended object. (See par. 341, as to Deeds.)

NOTE.—If the Trust Property be subject to heavy ground rent, the Committee is empowered to require more than two-thirds of the proposed outlay.

**335** The General Committee of Management is authorized to require that plans, specifications, and builders' tenders for any Chapel or other Trust Property, proposed to be built, shall be submitted for consideration. The sanction of the General Committee of Management, or of its Sub-Committee, is required for any expenditure over £20 beyond the amount of the contract originally sanctioned. (See par. 331, No. 7.)

N.B.—The entire cost of an organ shall be defrayed on or before the opening.

**336** In applications for permission to build, alter, repair, enlarge, or improve Chapels, no stipulation for any certain amount of grant shall be entered (except in the special case provided for in par. 331, No. 9). Applications for grants, if grants are desired, shall be presented afterwards on the proper "Form."

### V. INVESTIGATION BY DISTRICT COMMITTEE.

**337** Chairmen of Districts are required to make a full examination in the Annual District Meetings of the returns relating to every new Chapel, and other Trust Property, and all enlargements and purchases; and District Chapel Secretaries are required to forward all Schedules, Forms of Application, and Minutes of any other matter relating to Chapel affairs, so as to be with the Chapel Secretary not later than the 15th May.

**338** The Chairmen of Districts are also required to examine into all cases specially remitted to them, and to cause a record of the particulars to be made in the District Minutes, and the Minutes so made shall be read at each successive District Meeting until the case shall have been satisfactorily settled.

**339** Trustees violating any of our rules relating to Chapel affairs shall not receive assistance from the Chapel Fund, unless the Conference, upon a representation of the case by the General Committee of Management, shall authorize such assistance.

### VI. DEEDS.

**340** The attention of Superintendents is directed to the necessity of having all sites for new Chapels and other Trust Property duly settled by Trust Deeds. They are also required to make the earliest inquiry in relation to old Trust Deeds, and all other matters affecting the safety of our property, to take such steps as shall increase its security, and to afford the most reliable information in their Trust Schedules.

341 Heavy expenses for the settlement of Trust Property having been in some instances incurred for want of competent legal advice, the Conference directs that all Trustees, and Superintendents proposing persons to be Trustees, shall submit a draft of the intended Trust Deed to the General Committee of Management. (See Section on Trustees, par. 244.)

342 Suitable provision having been made for the custody of the Deeds and documents relating to Connexional Trust Property in the "Safe" in Dublin, and a Registrar of such Deeds and documents appointed, Superintendents are directed to urge upon Trustees the propriety of having their Deeds duly lodged with the Registrar.

In cases where Trustees choose to retain their Trust Deeds of Connexional property, instead of depositing them in the Connexional Safe, a memorial of such Title Deeds shall be sent to the Registrar for the purpose of securing uniformity and completeness in the Register.

343 District Chapel Secretaries in attendance at the Conference are directed to compare the District Chapel Register with the General Register, so as to have the former corrected and completely written up from year to year; when the District Chapel Secretary is not in attendance at the Conference, the Chairman of the District shall have a suitable person appointed to correct and complete the District Chapel Register, and each Chairman shall inquire at the Financial District Meeting whether the District Chapel Secretary's Book has been so compared with the General Register, and written up to date at the preceding Conference; special attention being directed to any Chapels transferred from one District to another.

**344** The Chairmen of Districts are directed to inquire at the Annual District Meetings whether the Circuit Schedule Books have been compared with the District Chapel Register, and written up to date.

### VII. MANAGEMENT OF TRUST PROPERTY.

**345** Suitable Cash and Minute Books shall be provided by the Officers of the Chapel Fund, and Trustees of each Chapel, or other Trust Property, are recommended to use the form of account books so provided. A Meeting of Trustees shall be held once in every year, at which the annual accounts of the Trust shall be audited. Minutes of Trustees' Meetings shall be taken and preserved. (See par. 237.)

**346** Superintendents are required to examine once a year the accounts of each Trust within their respective Circuits. Chairmen of Districts shall institute particular inquiry in the Annual District Meetings as to the observance of this direction.

**347** A Schedule duly filled up from the Circuit Book shall be forwarded every year, not later than the second Wednesday in April, by every Superintendent to the Chapel Secretary of his District. (See par. 232.)

(For other rules relating to Trust Property see Section on Trustees and Trustees' Meetings; pars. 235-243).

### VIII. INSURANCE OF CHAPELS, ETC.

**348** Superintendents are required to pay special attention to the Insurance of Chapels and other Trust Property against loss by fire; and it is directed that the amount covered by Insurance be entered in the Schedule, and the following question answered: Have the Premiums of Insurance for the current year been paid?

**349** The Chapel Fund Secretary shall, from year to year, report to the Conference all cases of uninsured Connexional Trust Property, and shall furnish the Chairman of each District with a list of uninsured Trust Properties in his District that inquiry may be made into each case at the Financial District Meeting.

N.B.—The Conference earnestly recommends to all Trustees of Chapels, or other Connexional Trust Property, that they should transfer their Fire Insurance business to the Wesleyan Methodist Trust Insurance Company.

### IX. LEGAL PROCEEDINGS.

**350** No lawsuit relating to Chapels, Schools, or other Trust Property, shall be commenced without the consent of the General Committee of Management, except by direction of the Conference; and unless such consent or direction be first obtained, the parties proceeding shall be alone responsible for all expenses incurred by such lawsuit.

### X. SALES.

**351** Every application for permission to sell Trust Property shall, after receiving the sanction of the District Meeting be submitted to the General Committee of Management for consideration. The case, if approved, shall be certified to the President of the Conference, who is authorized to affix his signature to any consent to the sale of Trust Property which may be thus certified to him as approved by the Committee.

All "Sales" which shall be duly sanctioned shall be entered in the Journal of the Conference.

DISTRICT CHAPEL SECRETARIES AND SUB-COMMITTEES.

**352** The following are the Rules relating to the appointment and duties of District Chapel Secretaries and Sub-Committees:—

1. A Chapel Secretary shall be appointed for each District, and Schedules for collecting all needful information shall be provided and sent to the Superintendents, who shall have them filled and returned to such Secretary in due time to be compiled and submitted to the Annual District Meeting.

2. The Chapel Secretaries shall be chosen at the Financial District Meetings, and in each case the name of the Minister chosen shall be forthwith transmitted by the Financial Secretary of the District to the Secretary of the Chapel Fund, who is required to furnish the District Chapel Secretary with a sufficient supply of Trust Property Schedules; such Schedules shall be forwarded by him to the several Superintendents of the District.

3. A Chapel Sub-Committee for the District shall be appointed at each Financial District Meeting, to consist of the Chairman of the District and the District Chapel Secretary, two other Ministers and four laymen. This Sub-Committee shall meet prior to the Annual District Meeting, shall examine the Schedules, and bring before the District Meeting any inquiries or suggestions arising out of such examination. The lay members shall be members of the District Meeting when Chapel affairs are under consideration.

4. Each District Chapel Secretary shall be provided with a book in which copies or abstracts of all Leases and Deeds of Trust belonging to the District shall be entered, for facility of reference and to avoid risk in transmitting by post the original documents. It is the duty of the District Chapel Secretary to see that all abstracts of Deeds relating to newly acquired property be duly entered in this Register, and that in these matters the information be accurate, and always kept up to date.

5. The Chapel Secretaries of the Districts are directed to

communicate with the Superintendents of Circuits in which are Trusts not legally settled according to the Conference plan, with the view of having the needful documents perfected and lodged with the Connexional Registrar.

6. A Tabular View of the Connexional Trust Property in the District shall be compiled by the District Chapel Secretary from the Circuit Trust Schedules, submitted to the Annual District Meeting, and its several particulars carefully considered. The totals for the District shall be entered in the Minutes. The Circuit Trust Schedules and the Tabular View, shall be copied by the District Chapel Secretary into the District Trust Schedule Book for the purpose of future reference and comparison, and shall be forwarded as early as possible after the District Meeting to the Secretary of the Chapel Fund.

7. The District Chapel Secretary shall call the attention of the Annual District Meeting to those cases in which from the absence of Deeds, from the state of repair, from the increase of debt, or from any other cause not previously under consideration, a special resolution of the District Meeting on the subject may be necessary.

## CHAPTER VI.

## THE HIBERNIAN AUXILIARY TO THE WESLEYAN METHODIST MISSIONARY SOCIETY.

### I. ORIGIN.

**353** The Hibernian Auxiliary to the Wesleyan Methodist Missionary Society originated in the following resolution of the Irish Conference adopted in 1813:—" Let Auxiliary Societies be established throughout all Ireland to raise annual Subscriptions for our Missions. Reports of the progress of the Missions, with accounts of the receipts and disbursements, together with the subscribers' names, shall be annually distributed among the subscribers. The Annual Collection for the Missions shall be regularly made in all our Congregations throughout Ireland."

### II. REGULATIONS CONCERNING THE COLLECTION AND TRANSMISSION OF FUNDS.

**354** A Committee shall be appointed by the Conference, comprising equal numbers of Ministers and Laymen of the Methodist Society, which shall superintend the collection of all money subscribed to the Hibernian Auxiliary in aid of the funds of the Wesleyan Methodist Missionary Society, and secure its transmission to the General Treasurers of the Parent Society in London, at the earliest period practicable.

# REGULATIONS FOR GRANTS FOR MISSIONS IN IRELAND.

**355** Two Treasurers shall be appointed by the Conference, a Minister and a Layman, who shall receive and transmit all money subscribed or bequeathed in Ireland in aid of the Parent Society, and who shall also receive the amount of the Annual Grant from the Committee of the Society for the work in Ireland, and disburse it to the Treasurers having charge of the Funds for carrying on the different departments of the work.

**356** A Secretary to the Hibernian Auxiliary Committee shall be appointed by the Irish Conference, who shall act as Convener, conduct the correspondence with the parent Committee, and perform such other duties as the Conference may appoint.

**357** The Circuit Treasurers are directed to forward to the Treasurers of the Committee in the first week in February, all collections or subscriptions which may have been received by them up to that date, to close their accounts for the year not later than the first of June, and to transmit the balance in their hands to the Treasurers of the Committee not later than the period at which the business of this department shall be transacted in the Conference.

The lists of subscribers for publication, corresponding in the totals with the remittances sent to the Treasurers, shall be forwarded to the Secretary of the Committee on or before the 10th of June. For lists received after that date, publication in the Report for the year cannot be claimed.

### III. REGULATIONS CONCERNING THE GRANT FROM THE PARENT COMMITTEE FOR MISSIONARY PURPOSES IN IRELAND.

**358** The Parent Committee shall determine from year to year the amount of money to be granted from the General Fund for expenditure on Missions and Schools in Ireland,

and before each year commences, shall declare the amount of grant for that year; and the Conference shall appoint a mixed Committee to determine from year to year in what proportions the grant shall be allocated to the different departments. The Committee so appointed, shall meet and report during the sittings of the Conference.

359 The Parent Committee shall have the right to appoint Visitors, either to the Committee of the Hibernian Auxiliary or to Mission Stations, to inspect and audit the accounts of the Treasurers, and to call for information from the Secretary, either in writing or otherwise, respecting the management and working of the Missions at any time it may judge expedient. This power includes the right of recommending to the Conference the appointment of a person, if at any time it may deem it necessary, for a sufficient period, to make a thorough investigation of the whole system and condition of Missions and Mission Schools, and to report thereon.

360 The Parent Committee shall be annually furnished with a report, comprising an account of the expenditure in detail, the number of Members and Scholars, Ministers and Teachers, together with a brief statement of the religious condition of all the Missions respectively.

361 The Irish Conference shall provide for the inspection and supervision of Mission and other Schools, according to what it may deem most conducive to the efficiency of the Schools.

### IV. MISSIONARY DEPUTATIONS.

362 The Representatives to the British Conference, from year to year, are instructed to communicate with the Secretaries of the Parent Committee with the view of having, at least, seven Ministers of the British Conference appointed to attend the Anniversaries of the Missionary Society in Ireland in the

following spring, in order to set forth and advocate the claims of the Society. An equal number of Ministers of the Irish Conference shall be appointed from year to year to assist in the deputation work on behalf of the Society.

363 The Committee shall prepare and publish in sufficient time, a Plan for the holding of Missionary Meetings in the principal Circuits throughout the kingdom; arranging the dates on which the Meetings are to be held and the Members of the Deputation who are to attend them. Suggestions may be sent from the Financial District Meetings to the Secretary of the Committee, with reference to any change or addition of places within the District which it is thought should appear in the following Plan.

N.B.—The expenses of the Members of the Deputation shall be paid by the Treasurers of the Hibernian Auxiliary

## CHAPTER VII.

## TRUSTEES FOR BEQUESTS.

364 Whereas it has been reported to the Conference that several Bequests have been made of various sums of money, for the purpose of assisting in the support of the Ministry in connection with various Circuits or Congregations, and for other purposes; and that in some cases no special provisions have been made by the testators for the proper investment of such Bequests and the due appropriation of the proceeds; and whereas it is inconvenient and unnecessary to create separate Trusts in each of those several cases, or in other like cases which may hereafter arise:—

The Conference resolves:—

1. That it is now expedient to appoint a Board of Trustees for Circuit and Connexional purposes, whose duties and responsibilities shall be defined and limited by such a duly executed Deed as the Conference may approve of.

2. That to this Board of Trustees shall be committed:—

(1.) Such sums of money as may from time to time be given or bequeathed for Circuit or Connexional purposes, for the investment and appropriation of which no distinct provision has been made by the donors or testators.

(2.) Such sums as Executors, or other persons having the control of them for such purposes, may desire to commit to such Trustees for safe investment and due appropriation, and which the Trustees may judge it expedient to accept.

(3.) Such sums as the Conference, or any Committee of the Conference, may from time to time direct.

3. The Conference approves of the Draft of a Trust Deed for the foregoing purposes, which has been read to the Conference.

4. It is desirable that Superintendents of Circuits communicate full information to the Secretary of the Board of Trustees concerning all Donations and Bequests for Circuit or Connexional purposes in their respective Circuits.

(For names of Trustees, with their Treasurers and Secretary, see the Annual Minutes of Conference.)

# CHAPTER VIII.

## EDUCATIONAL INSTITUTIONS AND COMMITTEES.

### I. SUNDAY SCHOOLS.

**365** The Conference has resolved that a Committee shall be appointed from year to year, consisting of an equal number of Ministers and Lay Gentlemen, with the President, the Vice-President and the Secretary of the Conference, and the Treasurers and the Secretary of the General Education Fund as *ex-officio* Members, to which all information relative to Sunday Schools within their Districts shall be forwarded by the District Educational Secretaries, (appointed as hereafter provided, see par. 375.) The Committee shall present an Annual Report to the Conference of the Statistics of the Sunday School Work throughout the several Districts, and of the spiritual results, or other matters of interest in connection with it, together with any suggestions for the better carrying on of the work, which the Committee may have to offer.

**366** A grant shall be made from the General Education Fund to meet the expenses of the Committee, and to enable the Committee to print the Statistics of all the Schools, and circulate them amongst the Ministers and Sunday School Superintendents.

**367** The Conference directs that the afternoon and evening of the Saturday after the Representative Session of the Conference assembles, shall be left free for a Sunday School Convention.

(For the Rules and Regulations affecting Sunday Schools, and Circuit Sunday School Committees, and Teachers' Meetings, see Part I., Chapter VII., pars. 249—256.)

## II. GENERAL EDUCATION—PRIMARY DAILY SCHOOLS.

### 1. *Origin of the Fund.*

**368** The General Education Fund originated in the movement set on foot in 1855 for "the increase of Wesleyan Agency in Ireland"; one of the resolutions then adopted being "that considering the extreme importance of bringing the children of the poor in Ireland under the influence of a Scriptural training in Schools conducted by spiritually minded men, in the employment of the proposed Fund special attention should be paid to the extension of Scriptural Schools, particularly among the neglected and the poor."

For more than thirty years previously Day Schools had been in operation, in connection chiefly with Mission Stations, and the Conference had been fully alive to the importance of augmenting the number of such Schools as a valuable auxiliary to the work of the Ministry. In the Centenary year encouraging aid was given by the appropriation from the Centenary Fund of £6000, the annual proceeds of which were to be applied to the maintenance of School Buildings; but though resolutions were from time to time adopted by the Conference and Committees of inquiry appointed, no very great progress had been made in promoting the establishment of new Schools until after the Conference of 1855.

In 1858 in the allocation of the "Fund for the increase of Wesleyan Agency" a sum of £3000 was the proportion of the anticipated sum of £21,000 which was allotted "for the promotion of General Education in Ireland," and a Committee was appointed to see to the application of the Fund in the erection or repairs of School-houses, the training of Teachers, and the providing of School-requisites and other matters incident to the work. In the following year the Conference resolved that its Ministers should be "at liberty to connect Schools under their patronage with the National Board of Education as *non-vested Schools*," and the General Education Committee was charged with the duty of such correspondence with the Commissioners, or other parties, as might be necessary in the carrying out of this resolution. In 1860 the Conference, in its desire for the increase of Day Schools, further resolved that "a public collection shall be annually made in all our Circuits and Mission Stations" in aid of the General Education Fund.

During this time, and for several years after, a distinction was kept up between the old established "Mission Schools" and the schools sustained by the General Education Fund; but in 1871 this distinction was discontinued; the "Grant" from the Committee of the Wesleyan Methodist Missionary Society for Mission work in Ireland was made direct to the Irish Conference, and the portion of the "Grant" annually spent upon "Mission Schools" was allocated to the Committee of General Education, and common provision was made for the aiding, inspection, and supervision of all the Schools.

## 2. *General Rules.*

**369** The Fund shall be termed "The General Education Fund," and shall consist of: (1) The sums contributed at the Annual Collections on behalf of the Fund in the several

Chapels; (2) The interest on the Centenary Grant "for the maintenance of School-buildings"; and (3) the sum annually allocated to the Education department from the Grant of the Committee of the Wesleyan Methodist Missionary Society for Mission work in Ireland. (See par. 355.)

370 The Fund shall be administered under the direction of the General Committee of Management subject to such Rules as the Conference shall from time to time adopt. A Report of the proceedings of the Committee in relation to the Fund shall be presented annually to the Conference.

371 The officers of the Fund shall be two Treasurers, a Minister and a Layman, and a Secretary, appointed annually by the Conference. The Treasurers shall keep the accounts of the Fund in a Bank in their joint names, and shall present to Auditors nominated by the Committee and appointed by the Conference a statement of the Income and Expenditure of the Fund, ending with the March quarter in each year. The Secretary shall conduct the necessary correspondence and prepare the Annual Report.

372 All applications to the General Committee of Management for grants for Teachers' Salaries, Building, Repairs, School Requisites, Books, or for any other purpose, should be made on the proper "Form" to be obtained from the Secretary of the Fund; and such applications must be approved of by a Quarterly and a District Meeting.

373 No grant for Rent shall be forwarded by the Treasurers unless applied for on the "Form" supplied by the General Committee on application to the Secretary; and no grant for Building or for Repairs shall be paid by the Treasurers until a certificate has been received by the Secretary on a "Form" to be supplied, on application to him, certifying that the work for which the grant was made has

been properly done, and the conditions annexed to the grant, if any, complied with.

**374** The General Committee reserves to itself the power of withdrawing its aid from any School in which its directions are not observed.

### 3. *District Education Secretaries, &c.*

**375** An Educational Secretary shall be appointed at each Financial District Meeting, who shall collect the statistics of the District as to Day Schools, and present them in a tabulated form to the Annual District Meeting. All Minutes affecting Day Schools should be forwarded immediately afterwards by the *District Secretary* to the Secretary of the Fund.

**376** The General Committee of Management shall supply a book for Reports and Statistics to each District Educational Secretary.

N.B.—The Schedules of Day Schools shall be submitted to the March Quarterly Meeting of the Circuit making the returns. (See Section on Quarterly Meetings par. 231, No. 11.)

### 4. *Visitation, Inspection and Examination.*

**377** The Schools shall be systematically visited by the Ministers of the Circuit or Mission wherein such Schools are situated; the pastoral visitation of the Schools shall be the subject of conversation and regulation at the Financial District Meetings, and at the Annual District Meetings inquiry shall be made as to the observance of the arrangement.

**378** Proper arrangements shall be made at the Financial District Meetings for the Inspection of the Mission Schools within the limits of each District, and for the visitation of the National Schools, and reports of the results shall be furnished in writing at the Annual District Meetings, such reports to be forwarded immediately to the Secretary of the Fund by the Secretary of the District.

379 Examination Papers in Religious Instruction prepared by the Officers of the Fund, shall be employed by Examiners who shall be selected by the Financial District Meeting. The course of study shall be printed in the Annual Report.

The Managers of Schools are requested to communicate, as early as possible, with the District Examiners, regarding the Schools to be examined, and the probable number of Pupils to be presented in each Division.

(The First and Second Classes, according to the National Board arrangement, shall form Division I. The Third and Fourth Classes shall form Division II. *These Divisions shall be examined* ORALLY. The Fifth and Sixth Classes shall form Division III.)

The Examinations should be held as early in March as convenient.

5. *Rules as to Management.*

380. The following are the Rules with reference to the Management of Schools, aided by Grants from the Fund (whether Mission Schools or National Schools), which have been adopted by the General Committee of Management, and sanctioned by the Conference :—

1. The Superintendent of the Circuit in which such School is situated is *ex-officio* Manager of the School; except in such cases as may be otherwise determined by the said General Committee.

2. The powers of a Manager in a Mission School shall be the same as in a National School, except where otherwise provided by these Rules.

3. The Manager has power to engage and to dismiss

Teachers, subject, in all cases, to the approval of the General Committee of Management.

4. In all cases Teachers are to be engaged on the "Memorandum of Agreement." provided by the General Committee of Management.

5. It is recommended to Managers of National Schools and to Local Committees to endeavour to secure, when practicable, the benefits of the Acts of Parliament passed with a view to providing residences for Teachers. The Commissioners of National Education will pay one half of the instalments payable to the Board of Works on account of "Loans" obtained for this purpose; and the General Committee of Management is authorized to direct the payment of the other half from the General Education Fund; deducting, in ordinary cases, the amount so paid from the "Grant for Supplemental Salary." The Treasurers of the Fund are authorized, if necessary, to become sureties to the Board of Works for the repayment of the "Loans."

6. The General Committee of Management, reserves to itself the power, after consultation with the Manager or Managers interested, to remove any Teacher from one School to another where such a removal may be deemed necessary or expedient. In any case in which a Teacher is removed at his own request, the Committee will not consider itself bound to pay his removal expenses; every other case of removal is to be determined on its merits by the Committee.

7. The course of instruction in Mission Schools shall be the programme of the National Board, unless in such exceptional cases as the General Committee of Management, for special reasons, may sanction another. The Register, Daily Report Book, and Class Roll, shall also be kept as in National Schools.

8. The Rules known as the Practical Rules of the National Board are to be adopted in all Mission Schools so far as may be consistent with the rules of the General Committee of Management.

9. The Religious Instruction in all Mission Schools, and of all Methodist pupils in National Schools, shall be given in accordance with the Manager's arrangement, and shall be given for at least half-an-hour daily during every day on which the School is open. The books to be used are the Bible, the Methodist Hymn Book, and the Methodist Catechisms. In the case of Model Schools the Superintendent of the Circuit in which the School is situated shall make arrangements with the authorities of the School for giving Religious Instruction to the Methodist pupils.

10. Each Teacher shall forward a quarterly return of his School, through the Manager, to the Secretary of the General Education Fund.

### III. WESLEY COLLEGE, DUBLIN.

381 In 1839 a Committee was appointed by the Conference to meet certain gentlemen for consultation concerning the desirableness of establishing a Proprietary Grammar School. A plan to effect this object was submitted to the Conference and approved of. Resolutions providing for the carrying out of this plan were adopted by the Conference of 1845; in 1846 the Institution was established under the name of "The Wesleyan Connexional School," and a Minister was appointed to the office of Governor and Chaplain. Provision was subsequently made for the education of a certain number of Ministers' Sons at this Institution, and this arrangement still continues. (See par. 315 (3.) The original Trust Deed has been superseded by a new one executed in 1878.

**382** In 1879 the Institution was removed to new premises, and was designated Wesley College. The premises are vested, and must always be vested, in eighteen Trustees, one half of whom shall be Ministers in Full Connexion with the Conference, and the other half Laymen, Members of the Methodist Church, residing in Ireland or elsewhere in the United Kingdom.

**383** The Committee of Management shall be appointed by the Conference and shall consist of ten persons (in addition to the Trustees for the time being) five of whom shall be Ministers, and the remaining five Lay Gentlemen, who shall be either Members or stated Communicants in the Methodist Church.

**384** The Committee of Management shall have the right of nominating persons to fill the respective offices of Governor and Chaplain, and of Head Master; but the appointment shall be with the Conference, and shall be for such time, and on such conditions, as the Conference may think proper.

**385** The Committee of Management shall have the entire management and control of the working of the Institution, shall fix the scale of fees and other charges, shall arrange and determine upon the course of study, and shall from time to time (subject, however, herein to the approval of the Conference) draw up and frame and promulgate such rules and regulations for the better management, supervision, and control of the Institution, as to them shall appear necessary, proper, or expedient.

**386** The Trustees shall prepare an Annual Statement of Accounts, and shall submit such statement to the Conference at each Yearly Meeting, together with the Report of the Committee of Management as to the general state and working of the Institution.

## IV. METHODIST COLLEGE, BELFAST.

### 1. ORIGIN AND DESIGN.

387   This College was originally intended to meet the increased necessity for higher education felt by the Methodists of Ireland, by providing in a new institution an enlargement of the purposes of the Connexional School in Dublin, embracing the training of Theological Students, and the education of sons of our Ministers.   It was erected and endowed by means of contributions received mainly from Methodists in Ireland, England and America, amounting in the aggregate to nearly £60,000.   It was vested in Trustees under the control of the Irish Methodist Conference by a Deed, setting forth the purposes of the trust, and providing for the management of the institution, and was opened for the reception of students and pupils on the 19th day of August, 1868.

388   After a period of twenty years the College was, under the Act of 48 and 49 Vic. c. 78, placed under the management of Governors, who, by the Scheme of the Commissioners of Educational Endowments (Ireland) No. 16, 18th May, 1888, were constituted a Body Corporate by the name of "The Governors of the Methodist College, Belfast," with perpetual succession and a common seal.   This Scheme has the force of an Act of Parliament, and while maintaining the authority of the Conference and providing for all the original purposes, gives to the Governors enlarged powers, including provision for the education of girls and for carrying into effect the munificent purposes of the late Sir William M'Arthur, K.C.M.G., in the erection and endowment of "The

M'Arthur Hall," which is intended to be a place of residence for daughters of Methodist Ministers and other female students or pupils of the College.

**389** The design is comprehensive, embracing the COLLEGE and the SCHOOL. The College receives two classes of students:—Accepted Candidates for the Ministry, in connexion with the Methodist Conference in Ireland; and Undergraduates of the Royal or any other University, who may attend Lectures in the Queen's College and have at the same time the advantages of a Christian home with aid in the study of their University course and careful religious instruction. The School has two departments—Boys and Girls—providing for the education of each at every age, from tender years till they are fully prepared for entering into commercial or collegiate life.

### II. SCHEME OF MANAGEMENT.

**390** The following is an abstract of the provisions in the Scheme of Management so far as they relate to the action of the Conference:—

#### 1. *Governing Body*.

The Governing Body shall be formed in the manner following—

1. It shall consist of six *ex-officio* Governors, and of elected Governors, who shall in the first instance be such and so many of the persons (not being qualified as *ex-officio* Governors), being the Trustees and Members of the Committee of Management of the College appointed by the Conference at its yearly meeting in the year 1887, as at the date of this Scheme shall be still acting as such. The number of the elected Governors shall ultimately be reduced to nineteen persons, who shall be appointed by the Conference as hereinafter provided.

The following persons shall be the *ex-officio* Governors:—
The Vice-President of the Conference, the Secretary of the Conference, the President of the College, the lay treasurer of the Home Mission Fund, the lay treasurer of the Children's Fund, and the lay treasurer of the General Education Fund, all of the Methodist Church in Ireland, and all for the time being.

2. The Governors shall constitute a Body Corporate by the name of "The Governors of the Methodist College, Belfast," with perpetual succession and a common seal, and power to acquire and hold property, real and personal, for all or any of the purposes of this Scheme, or for any other educational purpose of or connected with the College.

3. Such persons only shall be eligible to or qualified for the office of Governor as shall be either Ministers in connexion with the Methodist Church, or shall profess themselves members thereof. Whenever any Governor for the time being, having been at the time of his appointment as a Governor a Minister in connexion with the said Church, shall cease to be, or to be recognised as a Minister in connexion therewith, he shall thereupon vacate his office of Governor. The Governors shall at all times consist, as nearly as may be, of equal numbers of Ministers in connexion with the said Church, and of lay members of the same, and in every election or appointment of a Governor regard shall be had and effect given, as far as possible, to this provision.

4. At each yearly meeting of the Conference the elected Governors shall vacate their office, but every outgoing Governor shall be eligible for re-election. The Conference shall at each yearly meeting elect nineteen duly qualified persons to be the elected Governors for the ensuing year; provided that, so long as any of the first elected Governors herein named shall remain eligible and shall have been con-

tinuously re-elected from year to year, the Conference may re-elect such and so many of them as it shall think fit, but so that the total number of elected Governors shall not at any election be increased beyond the number of such first elected Governors then re-elected, with one other Governor for every three first elected Governors who shall have then ceased to be eligible, or shall not have been continuously re-elected from year to year.

5. Whenever any elected Governor shall die, or resign by writing under his hand, or become bankrupt, or refuse to act or become incapable of acting, or shall permanently cease to reside in Ireland, or shall cease to profess himself a member of the Methodist Church, his office shall thereupon become vacant, and the fact of every such vacancy with the cause thereof shall be recorded in the Minutes of the Governors, and shall be by them reported to the Conference at its next yearly meeting.

6. Whenever the number of elected Governors shall from any cause be reduced below nineteen, the remaining Governors for the time being may co-opt such and so many duly qualified persons to be Governors as may be required to make up the number of nineteen elected Governors, but every Governor so co-opted shall hold office only until the yearly meeting of the Conference next after his appointment.

7. At any time and from time to time after the date of this Scheme, the Conference may *alter the constitution of the Governing Body* hereby constituted in such manner as such Conference shall deem expedient, and may define the qualification, and provide for the election, co-option, or appointment of the Governors, other than *ex-officio* Governors, and may declare and define the office or offices which shall qualify any *ex-officio* Governor or Governors; provided that

the number of *ex-officio* Governors shall not at any time exceed eight, and that the number of Governors, other than *ex-officio* Governors, shall not at any time be less than eight, and that the total number of Governors shall not at any time be reduced below sixteen.

## 2. *Application of the Endowments.*

Amongst other objects specified, the Endowments are to be applied—

1. To provide and afford by means of a Theological Department of the College, subject to such fees, charges, terms and conditions as may from time to time be fixed by the Governors, board and residence, with theological and ministerial instruction and training in such subjects and according to such course and system of education as to the Governors (subject to the approval of the Conference) may from time to time seem expedient, to and for such and so many divinity students, being Candidates for the ministry of the Methodist Church, as may from time to time be elected or designated for such purpose by the Conference.

2. To provide and afford, subject to such fees, charges, terms and conditions as may from time to time be fixed by the Governors, board and residence, with instruction in the principles of the Christian religion, and education in the Greek, Latin and French languages, in mathematics, and other subjects of a general and liberal intermediate education, and in all such other languages, arts, sciences and subjects as to the Governors may from time to time seem expedient, to and for such and so many sons of Ministers of the Methodist Church as may from time to time be elected or designated for such purpose by the Conference ; and to apply for the benefit of such pupils, or towards the cost of their education and

maintenance, such funds as may from time to time be provided by the Conference or otherwise for that purpose.

3. To provide and afford, subject to such fees, charges, terms and conditions as may from time to time be fixed by the Governors, board and residence, with instruction in the principles of the Christian religion, in the subjects of a general and liberal intermediate education, and in all such other languages, arts, sciences and subjects as to the Governors may from time to time seem expedient, to and for such and so many daughters of Ministers of the Methodist Church as may from time to time be elected or designated for such purpose by the Conference, and to apply for the benefit of such pupils, or towards the cost of their education and maintenance, such funds as may from time to time be provided by the Conference or otherwise for that purpose.

### 3. *Religious Instruction.*

All students and pupils of the college, or of any department thereof, who shall reside in the college for all or any of the purposes aforesaid, shall there, and during their residence therein, receive religious instruction from the professors, lecturers, and other teachers thereof from time to time appointed by the Governors to give such instruction; and all such resident students and pupils shall be required to attend Divine worship, and to attend the classes or lectures from time to time appointed by the Governors for the purpose of affording such religious instruction; provided always, that the religious instruction to be given in the College shall be in conformity with the principles and doctrines of the Methodist Church, and no religious doctrines whatsoever shall be taught or promulgated in the College, except doctrines in strict conformity with the doctrines of the late Rev. John Wesley, as contained in his Notes on the New Testament, and in the first four volumes of his sermons (being the sermons commonly called and known as the Sermons of the Rev. John Wesley,) nor shall any catechisms whatsoever, for the purposes of religious instruction, be used or be permitted to be used at the said classes or lectures, or in any preparation therefor, or in any other form or mode of religious instruction, except such catechisms as have been published or may hereafter be published with the sanction of the Conference.

### 4. *Site for place of Worship.*

If and whenever sufficient funds shall have been provided, or shall be available, for the purpose, the Governors may, with the previous sanction of the Conference, set apart a sufficient quantity of the lands included in the endowments and adjacent to the College as a site for the erection of a suitable and convenient place of Divine worship in connexion with the Methodist Church for the use of the members of the said Church resident in the College and others.

### 5. *Scholarships and Exhibitions.*

The Governors (subject to the approval of the Conference), whenever it shall seem to them proper and expedient, shall and may determine upon scholarships and exhibitions to be founded in connexion with the College and provided out of the endowments; and shall and may direct and determine the departments or classes from which scholars or exhibitioners are to be elected or taken, and shall and may determine upon the course of study and examinations for such scholarships and exhibitions, and the duration and amount thereof and the conditions upon which the same shall be awarded and held. Subject to the approval of the Conference, the Governors may provide that such scholarships and exhibitions shall be tenable either at the College or at any university or other place of academical, professional, or technical education, and that the same shall be awarded and held either in money or by way of free education, or education at a reduced cost, or in such other mode as the Governors may consider most advantageous.

### 6. *President, Head Master, and Treasurer.*

The Governors shall in each and every year after the date of this Scheme, preparatory to the yearly meeting of the Conference, appoint or re-appoint a fit and proper person, being a Minister in connexion with the Methodist Church, to the office of President of the College, and another fit and proper person to the office of Head Master of the College. Each and every person so appointed or re-appointed shall (subject to suspension, deprivation, or dismissal by the Governors for such cause as they shall deem adequate) hold his office from the date of the confirmation of his appointment or re-appointment as hereinafter mentioned, for the term of one year then next ensuing, and thenceforward from year to year until some other person shall have been appointed in his stead. Provided always, that no appointment or re-appointment (save only in the case of any temporary appointment, as mentioned in the Scheme) either of the President or of the Head Master, nor any direction by the Governors as to salary or otherwise concerning them, shall be final until the same shall have been submitted to and approved by the Conference. Provided also, that the Conference may reject any President or Head Master so appointed or re-appointed by the Governors, and may elect another qualified person in the place of any person so rejected, and every person so elected by the Conference shall hold office in the same manner as if his appointment had been made and confirmed in manner hereinbefore provided.

If and whenever any President shall cease to be a Minister in Full Connexion with the Methodist Church, he shall thereupon vacate his office, and a vacancy shall thereupon be considered to have occurred in such office in the same manner as if such President had then died.

The Conference, at each yearly meeting, shall appoint a fit and proper person to fill the office of Treasurer of the College for the ensuing year, for the purposes and with the duties and obligations mentioned in the Scheme.

7. *Special Provisions as to the Theological Department.*

1. Unless and until the Conference shall otherwise direct, the President of the College for the time being shall also hold the office, and shall bear the additional title of, Theological Professor. Subject to the control of the Governors, he shall be the Principal and shall have the direction of the Theological Department, and of all religious instruction given in the College, and shall act as the Chaplain or Minister thereof.

2. The Governors shall set apart for the purposes of the Theological Department, and for the benefit of the students therein, the several portions of the present endowments specified in that behalf, and may receive and hold therewith for the same or like purposes all such further and other endowments, moneys, and property as may have been or may be from time to time set apart for or given or devoted to the purposes of the Theological Department or for the benefit of the students therein by the Conference or by any other person or persons. The endowments so set apart received **and held shall** be administered by the Governors as a separate

fund, to be called the Theological Endowment Fund, and the principal or capital of the said Fund shall be held upon trust, and the income or annual produce thereof and all annual contributions thereto shall be applied, for the purposes of the Theological Department, or for the benefit of the students therein, in accordance with the directions of the Conference, and with any special trusts or directions for the time being lawfully affecting the same.

8. *Special Provisions for the Education and Benefit of Ministers' Daughters.*

The endowments set apart received and held for the education or benefit of the daughters of Methodist Ministers who shall be students or pupils of the College, shall be administered by the Governors as a separate fund, to be called the Ministers' Daughters' Endowment Fund, and the principal or capital of the said Fund shall be held upon trust and the income or annual produce thereof and all annual contributions thereto shall be applied, for the purposes aforesaid, in accordance with the directions of the Conference, and with any special trusts or directions for the time being lawfully affecting the same.

9. *Special Provisions as to the M'Arthur Hall or Residence House for Female Students.*

The expense of the erection and completion of the building or buildings to be called "The M'Arthur Hall," shall, in the first instance, be defrayed and borne, so far as such funds shall extend, by and out of the funds provided for that purpose by Sir William M'Arthur, K.C.M.G., the founder thereof, and afterwards out of such other endowments and funds as may be set apart for or given or devoted to the purposes thereof, or for the benefit of the students and pupils resident therein, by the Conference or by any other person or persons, and all such endowments and funds shall be held and applied by the Governors for the purposes aforesaid in accordance with the directions of the Conference, and such other special trusts and directions as may, for the time being, lawfully affect the same. The admission and reception of students and pupils into the said Hall, when completed, shall be from time to time regulated by the Governors, and such provision shall be made for the admission or reception of Ministers' daughters, free of charge or at reduced charges, as the Conference shall from time to time appoint.

10. *Powers of Visitation and Alteration of Trusts by Conference.*

Subject to the provisions of this Scheme, it shall be lawful for the Conference from time to time to appoint two or more persons, being members of the Conference, to visit the College, and to inspect the same, and to inquire into the management thereof, and into the discipline and order thereof, and into any matter of complaint or dissension alleged to exist therein, and into the nature and particulars of the education and instruction given thereat, and to examine into the accounts connected with the College and the Endowments or other funds belonging thereto, and to report to the Conference upon all or any such matters as aforesaid. Subject as aforesaid, it shall also be lawful for the Conference at any time, whether acting upon any such report as aforesaid or not, to take the management of the College and of the Endowments either wholly or partially into consideration, and to vary, alter, or rescind all or any of the by-laws and regulations theretofore at any time made or promulgated by the Governors, and to direct the removal or abatement of any abuse connected with the management of the College or Endowments or otherwise, and to rectify or remove any just cause of complaint or dissension existing therein. Subject as aforesaid, it shall also be lawful for the Conference from time to time, at any yearly meeting, subject to the restrictions hereinafter mentioned, by deed under the hand and seal of the person for the time being presiding at such Conference, attested by three or more members of the said Conference present at such yearly meeting, to alter, vary, or annul any of the provisions of this Scheme contained, and to enact and declare other clauses, provisions, and trusts in the place and stead of those so altered, varied, or annulled, or in addition to those herein contained. Provided that no alteration, variation, or change whatsoever shall at any time be so made in the purposes hereinbefore declared as those for which the College was established and is to be maintained, or to which the Endowments and Funds belonging thereto are to be applied; provided also that no such alteration, variation, or change shall be contrary to anything contained in the Act. Save as hereinbefore provided, every act, matter or thing which the Conference is by this Scheme authorized or empowered to do or sanction, may be done or sanctioned by resolution of a yearly meeting of the Conference, and may be evidenced and attested by writing under the hand of the person for the time being presiding and of two or more other members present at such yearly meeting.

(For full details of the Scheme of Management see the "Scheme" itself, copies of which may be obtained from the President of the College, or from the Secretary of the Governors.)

# CHAPTER IX.

# THE METHODIST ORPHAN SOCIETY AND THE FEMALE ORPHAN SCHOOL.

### I. THE ORPHAN SOCIETY.

#### 1. *Origin.*

391 On the recommendation of the Waterford District Meeting, the Conference of 1869 resolved to establish a Methodist Orphan Society, and appointed a Committee to draw up a Scheme for its constitution and management. The Conference received a report from this Committee in 1870, and in the following year adopted and published a code of Regulations. These are retained as the basis of the Society, and, together with Resolutions of Conference passed in subsequent years, are embodied in the following paragraphs:—

#### 2. *Name.*

392 This Society shall be called THE METHODIST ORPHAN SOCIETY.

#### 3. *Object.*

393 The object of this Society shall be to aid in the maintenance and education of Orphan children, one or both of whose parents shall have been connected with the Methodist Church in Ireland.

#### 4. *Admission to the benefit of the Society.*

**394** In selecting the Orphans, as a general rule, a preference shall be given by the Committee to children who have lost both parents.

**395** A form of application shall be issued by the Committee, and all applications shall be signed by the Minister in charge of the Circuit, and by two annual Subscribers to the funds of the Society of not less than £1 each, or two Collectors of not less than £1 each.

**396** All applications shall be recommended by the Quarterly Meeting of the Circuit to which the Orphans belong, in addition to the Subscribers required by the " Form of Application," and shall be approved by the Annual District Meeting.

#### 5. *Management of the Society.*

**397** The business of the Society shall be conducted by a Committee, annually appointed by the Conference, consisting of an equal number of Ministers and Laymen, together with two Treasurers and a Secretary.

**398** The Orphans taken under the care of the Society shall, for the present, be put to lodge in suitable Methodist families. Special attention shall be given to their health and moral and religious education ; it being understood that each child is placed under the supervision of the Superintendent of the Circuit, and shall be required to attend the Methodist public services, and, when practicable, the Methodist Sabbath and Day Schools.

**399** At the March Quarterly Meeting inquiry shall be made as to the state and circumstances of the Orphans under the care of the Society in the Circuit.

**400** A list of the Orphans in each Circuit, with full particulars as to the parties under whose care they are placed, shall be left by each Superintendent for his successor, with note as to the health, &c., of the children; and inquiry shall be made as to these entries at the Annual District Meeting. In the event of the death of any Orphan under the care of the Society, the Superintendent of the Circuit shall forward immediate notice to the Secretary, with any further particulars which the Committee ought to know.

**401** A sum not exceeding five pounds annually shall be allowed by the Committee for each child under their care. All claims upon the funds of the Society shall cease on the child attaining the age of fourteen. A portion of the income shall be annually reserved by the Committee, to be allocated in apprenticeship fees, or outfit grants, on the children being put to business.

**402** In order to raise the necessary funds, the Committee shall endeavour to promote the appointment of Collectors in each Circuit and Mission; and, when practicable, the formation of Auxiliary Associations.

## II. THE METHODIST FEMALE ORPHAN SCHOOL.

### 1. *Origin.*

**403** The late Solomon Walker, of the city of Dublin, in the year 1803, bequeathed certain sums of money "for the purpose of founding and supporting a Female Charity School in the City of Dublin, to be called the Methodist Female Orphan School," and a School was founded in pursuance of his will. In the year 1825 "a sum of £500 was allocated for the purposes of the said School out of the assets of the late Rev. John Barrett, Senior Fellow of Trinity College, Dublin." In addition to these bequests certain other benefactions have been since received for the purposes of the School, which together constitute an Educational Endowment within the meaning of "The Educational Endowments (Ireland) Act, 1885."

**404** In addition to the proceeds of the Endowments mentioned above, Voluntary Collections and Contributions have been received from Congregations and members of the Methodist Church, and from other friends, which have been applied in the maintenance of the School and in erecting the present School-house in Harrington Street, in the City of Dublin.

### 2. *Scheme of Management.*

**405** In the circumstances stated, the Commissioners under the Educational Endowments Act, after due enquiry, framed a Scheme for the future government and management of the School; and directed that the above named Endowments "shall be held, governed, managed and applied for the purposes, with the powers, under the conditions and provisions, and in the manner set forth" in the Scheme.

The following are the principal provisions:—

1. The Governors constitute a Body Corporate by the name of "The Governors of the Methodist Female Orphan School," with perpetual succession and a common seal, and power to acquire and hold property, real and personal, for the purposes of the Scheme.

2. The Chairman and the Financial Secretary of the Dublin District, the Governor of Wesley College and the Superintendent Minister of the Methodist Centenary Church, all for the time being, are *ex-officio* Governors.

3. The subscribers to the School of One Pound annually, or of Ten Pounds in one sum, are authorized, at a yearly meeting held for the purpose, to elect not more than five duly qualified Governors for the ensuing year.

4. The December Quarterly Meeting of any Circuit collecting or subscribing Ten Pounds a year for the purposes of the School is entitled to elect two duly qualified Governors for the ensuing year, and a third such Governor if the sum so collected shall amount to Twenty Pounds or upwards.

5. Persons subscribing One Pound annually or Ten Pounds in one sum for the purposes of the School, and resident within the City or County of Dublin, are qualified to be elected as Governors, and may be re-elected if they have attended not less than one-third of the meetings of the Governors held during the year.

6. The Conference may alter the constitution of the Governing Body in such manner as it may deem expedient, and may define the qualification, and provide for the election, co-option, or appointment of Governors other than the *ex-officio* Governors, and may declare and define the office or offices which shall qualify any *ex-officio* Governor or Governors; provided that every Governor, other than an *ex-officio* Governor, shall be a subscriber or contributor to the funds of the School, and that the number of Governors, other than *ex-officio* Governors, shall not be less than seven and that no existing Governor shall be removed without his own consent.

7. Children eligible for admission must be the lawful children of Protestant parents either or both of whom are dead ; must be, ordinarily, not less than eight or more than twelve years of age ; and must be of good character and conduct, and physically and intellectually fitted to take full advantage of the education given by the School. Residence may continue till the age of sixteen, or in special circumstances, till the age of eighteen. Elections of applicants for admission are not to be held oftener than once in each half year. Paying pupils may be admitted upon such terms as the Governors

shall think proper; but so that the provision for free pupils shall not be prejudiced thereby.

8. The children shall, under the care of the Matron, or some other responsible person, attend Divine Service at such place of worship as the Governors shall from time to time appoint, and shall receive such religious instruction as may be approved by the Governors.

### 3. *Resolutions of the Conference.*

**406** "Whereas a Scheme has been framed by the Educational Endowments (Ireland) Commission for the future government and management of the Educational Endowment in the City of Dublin known as 'The Methodist Female Orphan School'; and, whereas, that Scheme confers upon the Conference certain powers and privileges with reference to the constitution of the Governing Body of the Institution, it is resolved":—

1. "That the Conference hereby recognises the Methodist Female Orphan School as one of the benevolent Institutions of the Methodist Church in Ireland, and commends it to the continued liberality of the Christian public."

2. "The Governors of the Institution are requested to present to the Conference from year to year a statement of the accounts of the Institution; together with a list of the Governors for the time being."

# CHAPTER X.

## TEMPERANCE COMMITTEE.

**407** Having received the Report of a Committee appointed to inquire into the question of intemperance, and to consider by what means, in consistency with the unity and harmonious working of the Connexional System, the influence of Methodism may be most effectually employed for the remedy of this wide-spread evil; and it being recommended that a Committee be appointed from year to year, to be composed of Ministers and Laymen, to aid in the suppression of the prevailing and demoralizing vice of drunkenness, the Conference resolved that a Committee for this purpose should be annually appointed in accordance with this recommendation.

(For names of Committee see Annual Minutes of the Conference.)

**408** The Committee shall watch Legislation affecting the interests of Temperance; and if it considers that Connexional action should be taken, it shall suggest such action to the Committee of Privileges.

**409** In order to promote the interests of religion and the elevation of the masses, the Conference directs that more attention shall be given to Temperance Organization in harmony with the Methodist Connexional System.

**410** The Committee is authorized to organize and maintain a Connexional Band of Hope and Temperance Association, to collect information from our several Circuits and Stations with respect to Temperance work therein, and to report annually to the Conference.

**411** A question shall be inserted in the District Temperance Secretary's Circuit Returns, asking for an account of the amount of money expended on Temperance work on each Circuit.

**412** The Conference strongly recommends that a Sermon on the subject of Temperance shall be preached in all our congregations on the same Sunday as that appointed for the like purpose by the British Conference.

**413** The Conference directs the appointment of District Temperance Secretaries, who shall be chosen by the Financial District Meetings.

**414** The Conference adopts the following RULES FOR BANDS OF HOPE AND TEMPERANCE ASSOCIATIONS :—

### OBJECTS.

Bands of Hope are designed to educate the young in the principles and practice of Temperance.

It is a generally recognised fact that many young people do not unite themselves with the Christian Church, and it is believed that this is owing in no small degree to social drinking customs; it is proposed, therefore, to raise a barrier against the influence which these customs exert by the formation of Bands of Hope, whose specific object shall be to train young people in habits of *Abstinence from all Intoxicating Liquors*.

#### DECLARATION.

"I promise, by Divine grace, to abstain from the use of all Intoxicating Liquors as Beverages."

#### RULES.

1. All children who are capable of understanding the nature of the engagement into which they desire to enter, and whose parents have assented thereto, are eligible for membership.

2. Children who are not old enough to understand the declaration of membership, may be enrolled as members at the request, and on the responsibility, of their parents.

3. The Management of the Band of Hope and Temperance Association shall be entrusted to a Committee consisting of the Ministers of the Circuit, a Treasurer, Secretary, Registrar and Visitors.

4. The Superintendent of the Circuit or one of his colleagues shall be *ex-officio* President.

5. No society, however small its money transactions, should be without a Treasurer and properly kept books.

6. The Secretary, under direction of the Committee, shall keep the Minutes, make arrangements for meetings, conduct correspondence, and prepare reports.

7. The Registrar shall keep a record of officers and members, register attendance and admissions, and arrange with Visitors to look after absent members.

8. The Visitors should ascertain by visitation the cause of absence of any member, and the mind of the parents of those wishing to join the Society.

9. The Committee shall be elected annually from the members of the Band of Hope and Temperance Association, on the nomination of the Superintendent of the Circuit and with the approval of the Circuit Quarterly Meeting.

10. Band of Hope and Temperance meetings should be held regularly, and begin and end promptly at the time appointed. Ordinary meetings should not much exceed an hour in duration.

11. Every meeting should be opened and closed with devotional exercises. The addresses should be short and the style simple. Singing should be assigned an important place in every meeting.

12. It should ever be remembered that the sentiments and music introduced will linger in the memory, and influence the feelings and character through subsequent years; hence they should be pure, refined, and elevating. And as "the harvest answereth to the seed," the speakers and reciters should seek not only to interest and amuse, but also to instruct, and thus to build up character on the basis of Christian principle.

13. As the religious character of Bands of Hope and Temperance Associations will largely depend on their close connection with the Sunday School, they should be encouraged and promoted by the Superintendents and Teachers of the Schools with which they are associated.

14. The Band of Hope and Temperance Associations should be carried on in the spirit of faith and prayer; and the whole organization should be regarded as a means of winning souls for Christ.

# APPENDICES.

I.—MR. WESLEY'S DEED OF DECLARATION, OR DEED POLL.

II.—DIGEST OF THE MARRIAGE LAWS.

III.—THE LAW RELATING TO BURIALS.

# APPENDIX I.

## DEED OF DECLARATION, OR DEED POLL, OF THE REV. JOHN WESLEY.

TO ALL TO WHOM THESE PRESENTS SHALL COME, JOHN WESLEY, LATE OF LINCOLN COLLEGE, OXFORD, BUT NOW OF THE CITY-ROAD, LONDON, CLERK, SENDETH GREETING :—

WHEREAS divers buildings, commonly called Chapels, with a messuage and dwelling-house, or other appurtenances, to each of the same belonging, situate in various parts of Great Britain, have been given and conveyed, from time to time, by the said John Wesley, to certain persons and their heirs, in each of the said gifts and conveyances named, which are enrolled in his Majesty's High Court of Chancery, upon the acknowledgment of the said John Wesley (pursuant to the Act of Parliament in that case made and provided) upon Trust, that the Trustees in the said several Deeds respectively named, and the survivors of them, and their heirs and assigns and the Trustees for the time being, to be elected as in the said Deeds is appointed, should permit and suffer the said John Wesley, and such other person and persons as he should for that purpose from time to time nominate and appoint, at all times during his life, at his will and pleasure to have and enjoy the free use and benefit of the said premises, that he the said John Wesley, and such person and persons as he should nominate and appoint, might therein preach and expound God's Holy Word; and upon further trust, that the said respective Trustees, and the survivors of them, and their heirs, and assigns, and the Trustees for the time being, should permit and suffer Charles Wesley, brother of the said John Wesley, and such other person and persons as the said Charles Wesley should for that purpose from time to time nominate and appoint, in like manner during his life—to have, use, and enjoy the said premises respectively, for the like purposes as aforesaid; and after the decease of the survivor of them, the said John Wesley and Charles Wesley, then upon further trust, that the said respective Trustees, and the survivors of them, and their heirs and assigns, and the Trustees for the time being for ever, should permit and suffer such person and persons, and for such time and times, as should be appointed at the yearly Conference of the people called Methodists, in London, Bristol, or Leeds, and no others, to have and enjoy the said premises for the purposes aforesaid: and whereas divers persons have, in like manner, given or conveyed many Chapels, with messuages and dwelling houses, or other appurtenances, to the same belonging, situate in various parts of Great Britain, and also in Ireland, to certain Trustees, in each of the said gifts and conveyances respectively named, upon the like trusts, and for the same uses and purposes as aforesaid (except only that in some of the said gifts and conveyances, no life-estate or other interest is therein or thereby given and reserved to the said Charles Wesley); and, whereas, for rendering effectual the trusts created by the said several gifts or conveyances, and that no doubt or litigation may arise with respect unto the same, or the interpretation and true meaning thereof, it has been thought expedient by the said John Wesley, on behalf of himself as donor of the several Chapels, with the messuages, dwelling-houses, or appurtenances, before-mentioned, as of the donors of the said other Chapels, with the messuages, dwelling-houses, or appurtenances, to the same belonging, given or conveyed to the like uses and trusts, to explain the words "Yearly Conference of the people called Methodists," contained in all the said Trust Deeds, and to declare what persons are members of the said Conference, and how the succession and identity thereof is to be continued :—

Now, THEREFORE, THESE PRESENTS WITNESS, that, for accomplishing the aforesaid purposes, the said John Wesley doth hereby declare, that the Conference of the people called Methodists, in London, Bristol, or Leeds, ever since there hath been any yearly Conference of the said people called Methodists, in any of the said places, hath always heretofore consisted of the Preachers and Expounders of God's Holy Word, commonly called Methodist Preachers, in connexion with, and under the care of, the said John Wesley, whom he hath thought expedient year after year to summons to meet him, in one or other of the said places, of London, Bristol, or Leeds, to advise with them for the promotion of the Gospel of Christ, to appoint the said persons so summoned, and the other Preachers and Expounders of God's Holy Word, also in connexion with, and under the care of, the said John Wesley, not summoned to the said yearly Conference, to the use and enjoyment of the said Chapels and premises so given and conveyed upon trust for the said John Wesley, and such other person and persons as he should appoint during his life as aforesaid, and for the expulsion of unworthy and admission of new persons under his care, and into his connexion, to be Preachers and Expounders as aforesaid, and also of other persons upon trial for the like purposes ; the names of all which persons so summoned by the said John Wesley, the persons appointed, with the Chapels and premises to which they were so appointed, together with the duration of such appointments, and of those expelled or admitted into connexion or upon trial, with all other matters transacted and done at the said yearly Conference, have, year by year, been printed and published under the title of "Minutes of Conference."

AND THESE PRESENTS FURTHER WITNESS, and the said John Wesley doth hereby avouch and further declare, that the several persons hereinafter named, to wit [*here follow the names and descriptions of one hundred persons*] being Preachers and Expounders of God's Holy Word, under the care and in connexion with the said John Wesley, have been, and now are, and do, on the day of the date hereof, constitute the members of the said Conference, according to the true intent and meaning of the said several gifts and conveyances wherein the words Conference of the people called Methodists are mentioned and contained; and that the said several persons before-named, and their successors for ever, to be chosen as hereafter mentioned, are and shall for ever be construed, taken, and be the Conference of the people called Methodists. Nevertheless, upon the terms, and subject to the regulations hereinafter prescribed; that is to say :—

*First*—That the members of the said Conference, and their successors for the time being for ever, shall assemble once in every year, at London, Bristol, or Leeds (except as aftermentioned), for the purposes aforesaid; and the time and place of holding every subsequent Conference shall be appointed at the preceding one, save that the next Conference after the date hereof shall be holden at Leeds, in Yorkshire, the last Tuesday in July next.

*Second*—The act of the majority in number of the Conference assembled as aforesaid, shall be had, taken, and be the act of the whole Conference, to all intents, purposes, and constructions whatsoever.

*Third*—That after the Conference shall be assembled as aforesaid, they shall first proceed to fill up all the vacancies occasioned by death or absence, as aftermentioned.

*Fourth*—No act of the Conference assembled as aforesaid shall be had, taken, or be the act of the Conference, until forty of the members thereof are assembled, unless reduced under that number by death since the prior Conference, or absence as after-mentioned; nor until all the vacancies occasioned by death or absence shall be filled up by the election of new members of the Conference, so as to make up the number one hundred, unless there be not a sufficient number of persons objects of such election; and during the assembly of the Conference there shall always be forty members present at the doing of any act, save as aforesaid, or otherwise such act shall be void.

*Fifth*—The duration of the yearly assembly of the Conference shall not be less than five days, nor more than three weeks, and be concluded by the appointment of the Conference, if under twenty one days; or otherwise the conclusion thereof shall follow of course at the end of the said twenty-one days; the whole of all which said time of the assembly of the Conference shall be had, taken, considered, and be the yearly Conference of the people called Methodists; and all acts of the Conference during such yearly assembly thereof, shall be the acts of the Conference, and none other.

*Sixth*—Immediately after all the vacancies occasioned by death or absence are filled up by the election of new members as aforesaid, the Conference shall choose a President and

Secretary of their assembly out of themselves, who shall continue such until the election of another President or Secretary in the next, or other subsequent Conference; and the said President shall have the privilege and power of two members in all acts of the Conference during his presidency, and such other powers, privileges, and authorities, as the Conference shall from time to time see fit to entrust into his hands.

*Seventh*—Any member of the Conference absenting himself from the yearly assembly thereof for two years successively, without the consent or dispensation of the Conference, and be not present on the first day of the third yearly assembly thereof, at the time and place appointed for the holding of the same, shall cease to be a member of the Conference from and after the said first day of the said third yearly assembly thereof, to all intents and purposes, as though he were naturally dead. But the Conference shall and may dispense with or consent to the absence of any member from any of the said yearly assemblies for any cause which the Conference may see fit or necessary; and such member, whose absence shall be so dispensed with or consented to by the Conference, shall not by such absence cease to be a member thereof.

*Eighth*—The Conference shall and may expel and put out from being a member thereof, or from being in connexion therewith, or from being upon trial, any person member of the Conference, or admitted into connexion, or upon trial, for any cause which to the Conference may seem fit or necessary; and every member of the Conference so expelled and put out shall cease to be a member thereof, to all intents and purposes, as though he were naturally dead. And the Conference, immediately after the expulsion of any member thereof, as aforesaid, shall elect another person to be a member of the Conference, in the stead of such member so expelled.

*Ninth*—The Conference shall and may admit into connexion with them, or upon trial, any person or persons whom they shall approve, to be Preachers and Expounders of God's Holy Word, under the care and direction of the Conference; the name of every such person or persons so admitted into connexion or upon trial, as aforesaid, with the time and degrees of the admission, being entered in the Journals or Minutes of the Conference.

*Tenth*—No person shall be elected a member of the Conference who hath not been admitted into connexion with the Conference, as a Preacher and Expounder of God's Holy Word, as aforesaid, for twelve months.

*Eleventh*—The Conference shall not, nor may, nominate or appoint any person to the use and enjoyment of, or to preach and expound God's Holy Word in, any of the Chapels and premises so given and conveyed, or which may be given or conveyed, upon the trusts aforesaid who is not either a member of the Conference, or admitted into connexion with the same, or upon trial, as aforesaid; nor appoint any person for more than three years successively, to the use and enjoyment of any Chapel and premises already given, or to be given or conveyed, upon the trusts aforesaid, except ordained Ministers of the Church of England.

*Twelfth*—That the Conference shall and may appoint the place of holding the yearly assembly thereof, at any other city, town or place, than London, Bristol, or Leeds, when it shall seem expedient so to do.

*Thirteenth*—And for the convenience of the Chapels and premises already, or which may hereafter be, given or conveyed upon the trusts aforesaid, situate in Ireland, or other parts out of the kingdom of Great Britain, the Conference shall and may, when and as often as it shall seem expedient, but not otherwise, appoint and delegate any member or members of the Conference, with all or any of the powers, privileges, and advantages, herein-before contained or vested in the Conference, and all and every the acts, admissions, expulsions, and appointments whatsoever of such member or members of the Conference, so appointed and delegated, as aforesaid, the same being put into writing, and signed by such Delegate or Delegates, and entered in the Journals or Minutes of the Conference, and subscribed as aftermentioned shall be deemed, taken, and be the acts, admissions, expulsions, and appointments of the Conference, to all intents, constructions, and purposes whatsoever, from the respective times when the same shall be done by such Delegate or Delegates, notwithstanding anything herein contained to the contrary.

*Fourteenth*—All resolutions and orders touching elections, admissions, expulsions, consents, dispensations, delegations, or appointments, and acts whatsoever of the Conference, shall be entered and written in the Journals or Minutes of the Conference, which shall be kept for that purpose, publicly read, and then subscribed by the President and Secretary thereof for the time being, during the time such Conference shall be assembled, and when so entered and subscribed shall be had, taken, received, and be the acts of the Conference and such entry and subscription, as aforesaid, shall be had, taken, received, and be evidence of all and every such acts of the said Conference, and of their said Delegates, without the aid of any other proof, and whatever shall not be so entered and subscribed, as aforesaid, shall not be had, taken, received, or be the act of the Conference; and the said President and

Secretary are hereby required and obliged to enter and subscribe, as aforesaid, every act whatever of the Conference.

*Lastly*—Whenever the said Conference shall be reduced under the number of forty members, and continue so reduced for three yearly assemblies thereof successively, or whenever the members thereof shall decline or neglect to meet together annually for the purposes aforesaid, during the space of three years, that then, and in either of the said events, the Conference of the people called Methodists shall be extinguished, and all the aforesaid powers, privileges, and advantages shall cease, and the said Chapels and premises, and all other Chapels and premises, which now are, or hereafter may be, settled, given, or conveyed, upon the trusts aforesaid, shall vest in the Trustees for the time being of the said Chapels and premises respectively, and their successors for ever; UPON TRUST that they, and the survivors of them, and the Trustees for the time being, do, shall, and may appoint such person and persons to preach and expound God's Holy Word therein, and to have the use and enjoyment thereof, for such time, and in such manner, as to them shall seem proper.

PROVIDED ALWAYS, that nothing herein contained shall extend, or be construed to extend, to extinguish, lessen or abridge the life-estate of the said John Wesley and Charles Wesley, or either of them, of and in any of the said Chapels and premises, or any other Chapels and premises, wherein they the said John Wesley and Charles Wesley, or either of them, now have, or may have, any estate or interest, power or authority whatsoever. IN WITNESS WHEREOF, the said John Wesley hath hereunto set his hand and seal, the twenty-eighth day of February, in the twenty-fourth year of the reign of our Sovereign Lord George the Third, by the Grace of God, of

Great Britain, France, and Ireland, King, Defender of the Faith, and so forth, and in the year of our Lord one thousand seven hundred and eighty-four.

JOHN WESLEY.

Sealed and delivered (being first duly stamped) in the presence of
{
WILLIAM CLULOW, Quality Court, Chancery Lane, London.
RICHARD YOUNG, Clerk to the said William Clulow.
}

Taken and acknowledged by the Rev. John Wesley, party hereto, this 28th of February, 1784, at the Public Office, before me,

EDWARD MONTAGU.

# APPENDIX II.

## DIGEST OF THE MARRIAGE LAWS SO FAR AS THEY AFFECT THE MINISTERS AND MEMBERS OF THE METHODIST CHURCH IN IRELAND.

### I. REGISTRATION OF CHAPEL.

Before a Marriage can be solemnized in any Methodist Chapel, the Chapel must be duly registered for that purpose by the Registrar-General. The mode of obtaining such registration is as follows:—

The officiating Minister of the Chapel, or the Trustee or Owner, must certify in writing, signed by him, to the Registrar General that such building is used as a place of Public Worship by a Congregation of the Methodist Church. The Minister, Trustee, or Owner certifying, must at the same time deliver to the Registrar-General a certificate signed by ten householders that such Chapel has been used by them during one year, at least, as their usual place of Public Worship, and that they are desirous that such place should be registered for solemnizing Marriages therein, and such Minister, Trustee, or Owner shall counter-sign such certificate.

On the receipt of such certificate, the Registrar-General shall register such Chapel in the General Registry Office, and shall send a certificate of such Registration to the person certifying, and to the Registrar of the District in which the Chapel is situated.

The fee for such Registration, which must be paid at the time of delivery of the certificates to the Registrar-General, is one pound.

Should such Chapel be disused for the Public Religious Worship of the Congregation on whose behalf it was registered, the Registrar-General shall cause the Registration to be cancelled, provided that if it be proved to his satisfaction that the same Congregation use instead thereof some other such building for the same purpose, the Registrar-General may substitute and Register such new Place of Worship instead of the disused building, although such new Place of Worship may not have been used for that purpose during one year then next preceding.

Every application for the substitution and registry of a new Chapel or building in place of a disused one, shall be made to the Registrar-General through the Registrar of the District. After such cancelling or substitution shall have been made by the Registrar-General, it is not lawful to solemnize any marriage in such disused building. The fee for the substitution and registry is one pound, and is payable to the Registrar of the District.

## II. NOTICES AND DECLARATIONS PRELIMINARY TO MARRIAGE.

### 1. *Marriage by Special Licence.*

When the Marriage is intended to be by *Special Licence*, a "Form of Declaration" must be obtained from the Secretary of the Conference which must be properly filled by one of the parties intending Marriage, and subscribed before a Justice of the Peace. This declaration must set forth that there is "not any impediment of kindred or alliance, or other lawful hindrance to the Marriage"; that both the parties are "Members of the Methodist Church," and that both parties are of full age, or if either, not being a widower or widow, be a Minor under the age of twenty-one years, that the required "consent has been duly given and obtained" to the Marriage. (See page 185 for parties authorized to consent.) When the declaration is duly subscribed and attested, it must be returned to the Secretary of the Conference, who is then authorized to issue his *Special Licence* for the Marriage.

The consent which is required to the Marriage of a Minor should be in writing, and should be verified to the satisfaction of the Secretary before the Licence is issued.

### 2. *Marriage by Ordinary Licence.*

When the Marriage is intended to be by ordinary Licence obtained from the Registrar of the District, Notice must be served upon the Registrar by one of the parties, who must attend at his office for that purpose.

The Notice when filled up must contain the following particulars:—

The name and surname of each of the parties.

The condition of each, whether *Bachelor* or *Widower*, *Spinster* or *Widow*.

The rank, profession, or calling.

The age of each, thus, of *Full Age* or *Minor* as the case may be.

Their respective dwelling places, and the time during which each has dwelt therein. If the time is more than a month, it may be so stated.

The Chapel or Place of Worship which the parties usually attend, respectively.

The Chapel in which the Marriage is to be solemnized, which must be within the District of the Registrar—or, if the parties reside in different Districts, of one of the Registrars—to whom the Notice is given.

The party giving Notice is required to declare that there is no lawful impediment to the Marriage; that the parties have, for one month preceding, usually attended Divine Worship in the Chapel or building named in the Notice; that one of them has resided for *fifteen* days in the District of the Registrar on whom notice is served, and, in the case of Minors, that the necessary consent has been obtained.

If the parties intending Marriage reside in different Registrars' Districts, notice must be served on the Registrar of each District.

In cases where both parties reside in the same District, a residence of *fifteen* days is necessary for one party, and not less than *seven* days for the other; but if they reside in different Districts, a residence of *fifteen* days *in each* is necessary at the time of the service of the Notice.

When a Notice of intended Marriage is served on a Registrar, he is required, on the day on which he receives the Notice, or on the following day at the latest, to send by post in a registered letter, a copy of the Notice to the Minister of the Chapel stated in the Notice, as that in which the Marriage is intended to be solemnized, and also to the Minister of the Chapel or Place of Worship which the parties to the Marriage usually attend.

The Licence may be obtained from the Registrar on the eighth day from the day of entering the Notice, if the Marriage has not in the meantime been forbidden, or a Caveat entered against it. Before the grant of the Licence the Registrar is to administer to the party who served the Notice, in addition to the declaration previously made, an oath (or declaration if the party objects to take the oath) to the effect that there is not any lawful impediment to the Marriage; that one of the parties for *fifteen* days before the grant of the Licence has resided in the District in which the Marriage is to be solemnized; and that the parties are both of full age, or if not, that the necessary consent has been obtained.

If the parties reside in different Districts, a Certificate printed in red ink must be obtained from the Registrar of the other District, and delivered to the Registrar of the District in which the Marriage is to be solemnized before he can issue his Licence.

3. *Marriage without Licence upon production of a Registrar's Certificate.*

If instead of a Marriage by Ordinary Licence it is intended that the Marriage shall be without Licence upon the production of the Registrar's *Certificate*, Notice must be given to the Registrar in the same way, and embracing the same particulars as already noted in the case of Marriage by Licence.

In the case of Marriage by *Certificate*, the required term of residence in the District of each party before Notice is given is *seven* days instead of *fifteen*.

A declaration similar to that for Marriage by Licence, except as to length of residence, must be made at the time of giving Notice by the party serving the Notice.

On the *twenty-second* day from the day of entry of the Notice, a "Certificate," authorizing the Marriage, printed in black ink, may be issued by the Registrar if the Marriage has not been forbidden, or a Caveat entered against it.

If the parties reside in different Registrar's Districts, Notice must be given to the Registrar of each District, and a "Certificate" printed in black ink obtained from each Registrar.

#### 4. *Marriage in Ireland, where one of the parties resides in England.*

In such a case the party resident in England should serve Notice on the Superintendent Registrar of the District in which he, or she, resides and obtain his Certificate for Marriage by Licence which cannot legally be issued until after the expiration of *seven* days next after the day of entry of Notice.

After the expiration of seven days *from the issuing of such Certificate*, it may be produced to the Registrar in Ireland, upon whom Notice must have been previously served in the usual way required for Marriage by Licence, and he may then issue his Certificate, printed in red ink, and grant a Licence for Marriage.

#### 5. *Marriage in Ireland, where one of the parties resides in Scotland.*

The party resident in Scotland must procure from the Minister of the Congregation with which he, or she, has been connected for a month at least preceding, a Certificate that *banns* of the intended Marriage have been published in that Congregation on three different Sundays. From and after the expiration of seven days from the granting of such Certificate its production to the Registrar in Ireland will authorize him to issue his Certificate and grant Licence for the Marriage. Banns, however, can only be published in Scotland in the Established Church.

#### 6. *Marriage in England, where one of the parties resides in Ireland.*

The party resident in Ireland should serve Notice for Marriage without Licence on the Registrar of the District in which he or she resides. After *twenty-one* days the Registrar may issue his Certificate, printed in black ink, which should be produced to the Superintendent Registrar in England, within whose District the Marriage is to be solemnized and on whom Notice had been served by the other party.

Or, if it be convenient for the party usually resident in Ireland to proceed to England and arrive there *three* days before the day of the Marriage, the Marriage can be solemnized by Licence under the English Law, and Notice to the Registrar in Ireland will not be required.

7. *Marriage in Scotland where one of the parties resides in Ireland.*

The Irish Statutes contain no provision for such cases; and some doubt appears to exist as to the requirements of the Scotch law. Application should be made to the Session Clerk of the Parish in Scotland in which the Marriage is to be solemnized.

III. MEANS OF PREVENTING IMPROPER MARRIAGES.

In addition to the solemn Declaration which accompanies the serving of the Marriage Notice, and which precedes the issuing of the Licence, two other means are provided for preventing improper Marriages—1. By forbidding the issue of the Certificate; 2. By entering a Caveat.

Any of the persons whose consent to the Marriage of a Minor is necessary, may, without fee, forbid the issue of the Registrar's Certificate, by writing in the Marriage Notice Book the word "forbidden," and signing his or her name and place of abode, and the character in respect of which he or she is so authorized.

The persons authorized to give consent in the case of the Marriage of Minors are as follows:—

1. If both parents are living:—*The Father alone.*

2. If the Father is living and the Mother dead, she having previously nominated a Guardian, or Guardians, to act jointly with the Father, and such appointment having been confirmed by the Court after being satisfied as to the unfitness of the Father to be sole Guardian:—*The Father jointly with the Guardian, or Guardians, so nominated by the Mother and confirmed by the Court.*

3. If the Father is living and the Mother dead without having made any appointment so confirmed as aforesaid:—*The Father alone.*

4. If the Father is dead and has appointed no Guardian, or no Guardian has been appointed by the Court to act jointly with the Mother:—*The Mother alone.*

5. If the Father is dead and has appointed a Guardian, or if a Guardian, or Guardians, shall have been appointed by the Court to act jointly with the Mother:—*The Mother jointly with such Guardian, or Guardians.*

6. If the Parents are both dead and a Guardian, or Guardians, shall have been appointed by one of them only:—*The Guardian, or Guardians, so appointed.*

7. If the Parents are both dead and a Guardian, or Guardians, shall have been appointed by each:—*The Guardian, or Guardians, appointed by the Father and by the Mother, respectively, acting jointly.*

8. If a Guardian, or Guardians, shall have been appointed by the High Court of Justice to act without the intervention of any Parent, or to act when the Parents are deceased:—*The Guardian, or Guardians, appointed by the High Court of Justice.*

In the event of Guardians being unable to agree, any of them may apply to the court for its direction.

The High Court of Justice may remove any Guardian from his office and appoint another in his place.

Any person, on payment of a fee of five shillings, may enter a Caveat against the issue of the Registrar's Licence or Certificate. The Caveat must be signed by or on behalf of the person who enters it, and must state the ground of objection on which it is founded. Forms for the purpose are supplied on application. When a Caveat is entered, the Registrar shall not issue or grant any Licence or Certificate until he has examined into the matter and is satisfied that it ought not to obstruct the grant of the Licence or Certificate; or until the Caveat be withdrawn by the party who entered it. But caution must be exercised; as any person entering a Caveat on frivolous grounds is liable to an action.

As one object of the sending a copy of the Notice of Marriage to the Minister of the Chapel which the parties intending Marriage usually attend is evidently to assist in guarding against clandestine Marriages, it is incumbent on Ministers receiving such Notices to make sure that the parents or guardians, or near relatives, of the parties are not in ignorance of the intention of Marriage.

### IV. THE SOLEMNIZATION OF MARRIAGE.

The Marriage, if by *Special Licence*, may be solemnized at any convenient time at any place in Ireland within three Calendar months from the date of the Licence, by the Minister of the Methodist Church named in the Licence, or by any other Minister of the Methodist Church, according to the usages of the said Church.

The Licence should be delivered to the Officiating Minister previous to the Marriage.

Every Marriage by ordinary *Licence*, or, without Licence, on production of the Registrar's *Certificate*, must be solemnized in the Chapel named in the Notice; by a Minister of the Religious Denomination or Body to which the parties, or either of them, belong; between the hours of eight in the morning and two in the afternoon; with open doors; in the presence of two or more credible witnesses; and within three Calendar months from the date of the entry of the Notice in the Registrar's Marriage Notice Book.

The Licence or Certificate should be delivered to the Officiating Minister previous to the marriage.

No marriage can take place in a Methodist Chapel without the consent of the Minister, or of one of the Trustees; hence the necessity for the Registrar sending Notice of the intended Marriage to the Minister of the Chapel in which it is proposed to solemnize the Marriage. The Minister receiving such Notice should, if there be reasonable ground for objecting to the Marriage being solemnized in that Chapel, at once notify the persons concerned.

The Law requires that the Marriage must be solemnized by a Minister of the Church or Body to which the parties, or either of them, belong; which must also be the Body on whose behalf the Building was Registered. Marriages, therefore, in Methodist Chapels in Ireland can only be solemnized by a Methodist Minister in Full Connexion with the Conference; and at least one of the parties must be a member of the Methodist Church. *A Registered Building can only be used for the purposes of the Body on whose behalf it was Registered.*

V. REGISTRATION OF MARRIAGES AND QUARTERLY RETURNS.

The Registrar-General is required to furnish Duplicate Marriage Register Books for the use of the Officiating Minister of every Methodist Chapel, duly registered for the solemnization of Marriages. These Register Books are to be kept in the custody of the Minister in charge of that Chapel, and he is the person to receive the usual Notices and to make the usual Quarterly Returns. When the Books are filled one is to be deposited with the Registrar of the District.

N.B.—The Conference directs that in the case of two or more Ministers on a Circuit, the Minister residing most convenient to the Chapel shall be regarded as "the Minister in charge of the Chapel."

After a Marriage has been solemnized, upon the Registrar's Certificate by ordinary Licence, or without Licence on a Registrar's Certificate, the law requires that it be registered in each of the Duplicate Marriage Register Books, and a penalty of £40 is imposed upon any Minister who refuses, or, without reasonable cause omits to register any Marriage solemnized by him, or which he ought to Register. No other Books than those supplied by the Registrar-General can legally be used for the Registration of Marriages. Every entry in each Book must be signed by the Officiating Minister; by the parties married (the woman signing her Maiden Surname, or if a Widow, her last Married Surname); and by two witnesses.

In filling up the entries in the Marriage Register Book, great care should be taken by the Minister to ensure that the particulars in each entry correspond exactly in both Books; that none but good black ink be used; and that the writing be very clear and distinct so as to guard against mistaking names when copies of the Register are afterwards taken.

The Registration of a Marriage which has been solemnized under the authority of a *Special Licence*, is to be effected as follows:—A form of Certificate must be procured by one of the parties intending Marriage from the Registrar of the District in which the Marriage is to take place; this Certificate must be delivered to the Officiating Minister, who shall sign it after the celebration of the Marriage, and see that it is also signed by the parties married, and by two witnesses. The husband is bound to deliver this Certificate, or send it by post, to the Registrar-General within three days thereafter ; and in case of failure so to deliver or send the Certificate, he is liable to a penalty not exceeding ten pounds. Though the "Act" does not *require* that Marriages by *Special Licence*, even when they are solemnized in a Chapel registered for Marriage, should be registered in the duplicate Register Books in the usual way, yet it is highly convenient and desirable that they should be so registered, and it is the usual custom.

Every Minister having custody of the Marriage Register Books of any Chapel registered for Marriages, is bound to deliver or forward in the months of *April, July, October,* and *January* to the Registrar of the District in which the Chapel is situated, a true copy certified by him under his hand of all the entries of Marriages in the Register Book for the three months immediately preceding. If no Marriage has been celebrated within the Quarter for which the Return is made, a "Nil" Return should be filled and forwarded.

Forms of Return will be sent by the Registrar-General on application being made to the Registrar of the District. The Returns should be forwarded not later than the 15th of the month following the termination of each Quarter.

### VI. FEES.

The following Fees are payable to the parties and for the purposes mentioned :—

1. To the *Secretary of the Conference* for Special Licence, including the Stamp Duty of Five Pounds    £6 6 0
2. To the *District Registrar,* for entering Notice of Marriage      ..    ..    ..    ..    0 1 0

## MARRIAGE FEES.

For each Registered letter sent to the Minister of the Place of Worship attended by the parties, or to the Minister of the Chapel in which the Marriage is to be solemnized .. .. 0 1 0
    For Red Certificate preceding issuing of Licence 0 1 0
    For Licence .. .. .. .. 0 5 0
    For Certificate when Marriage is without Licence .. .. .. .. .. 0 1 0
    For entering a Caveat .. .. .. 0 5 0
    3. To the *Officiating Minister* .. ..

No Fee is provided by Statute, and no Fee is demanded; it is usual, however, for a Fee to be paid suitable to the condition in life of the parties to the Marriage.

    4. To the *Minister having custody of the Register Books*, for Stamped Certified Copy of entry of Marriage .. .. .. .. .. 0 2 7

---

NOTE—The foregoing "Digest of the Marriage Laws" has been submitted to the Assistant Registrar General and is approved by him as correct.

# APPENDIX III.

## THE LAW RELATING TO BURIALS.

In 1868 an "Act" was passed, entitled "An Act to amend the Law which regulates the Burial of Persons in *Ireland* not belonging to the Established Church;" of which the following are the principal provisions:—

"Whenever, after the passing of this Act, any person who at the time of his or her death shall not have been a member of and in communion with the United Church of *England* and *Ireland* shall be buried, as of right, within any Churchyard or Graveyard, the Soil or Freehold of which shall be vested in any Rector, Vicar, or other Incumbent, it shall be lawful for the Priest or Minister of the Religious Denomination to which such person shall have belonged at the time of his or her death, and he is hereby empowered, to attend such Burial and to read such Prayers or perform such Burial Service at the Grave in such Churchyard or Graveyard as is usual and customary at Burials of persons belonging to such Religious Denomination; and any person wilfully obstructing such Prayers or Burial Service shall be deemed guilty of a misdemeanour: provided always that such Prayers shall not be read nor such Burial Service performed, either wholly or in part, during the time of the Celebration of Divine Service or any Rite or Ceremony of the said United Church, or during the Catechising or other instruction of children or young persons in the Church or Chapel to which such Churchyard or Graveyard belongs; nor within half an hour before the commencement or after the conclusion of any such Celebration, Catechising, or Instruction; nor during the time at which the Incumbent or Minister of such Church or Chapel, or any other Minister or other Ecclesiastical person, shall be performing the Burial Service in such Churchyard or Graveyard; nor during the performance of any other Burial Service therein."

" Such Priest or Minister who may purpose to attend such Burial, shall, twenty-four hours before the reading of such Prayers, or the performance of such Burial Service, serve or cause to be served upon the person appointed by the Rector, Vicar, or other Incumbent of the Parish, to receive such Notice, a Notice in writing, signed with his name, stating the name and late residence of the person about to be buried, and the hour at which he purposes to read such Prayers or perform such Burial Service; and if there be no Celebration, Catechising, or Instruction already appointed to take place, or other Burial Service appointed to be performed at the time specified in the Notice, of which he is to be then and there informed, he shall read such Prayers or perform such Service at the time for which he has given Notice; but if any Celebration, Catechising, Instruction, or other Burial Service shall have been already appointed, then he shall appoint some other convenient time before or after such Celebration, Catechising, Instruction or other Burial Service."

---

The above first recited provision of the "Act" of 1868 applies to cases where persons not belonging to the United

Church of *England* and *Ireland* " shall be buried, as of right," and the question necessarily arose, to whom did that "right of burial" belong? Moreover, the passing of the "Irish Church Act" of 1869 made important changes in the law in other respects, and the question arose whether the Burial Law of 1868 was affected thereby. In 1878 a " case " bearing upon these points was submitted to the Solicitor General of that day, and the following is his " opinion ":—

" The Act 31 and 32 Vic. cap. 103 refers to and deals with Churchyards or Graveyards attached to, or belonging to Parish Churches, which were vested before the Irish Church Act in the Incumbent of the Parish. The " right of burial " in such Graveyards or Churchyards belonged at the time of the passing of that Act, *primâ facie*, to every resident in the Parish, who died therein. I am also of opinion that every person who died in the Parish, even although he had not a residence there, was entitled, *primâ facie*, to be buried in such Graveyards or Churchyards : but a person who usually resided in the Parish, but did not die there, was not entitled to such right of burial, although such person might be buried therein with the permission of the Incumbent. Such was in my opinion the right of burial that *primâ facie* existed in the Graveyards referred to ; and as regards the great majority of such cases, I have no doubt that such *primâ facie* presumption could not be refuted, and that the persons whom I have mentioned were actually entitled to bury therein as of right."

" I am of opinion that the rights of burial as they existed at the time of the passing of the Act 31 and 32 Vic. cap. 103, have not been affected by the Irish Church Act. The same classes of persons who were entitled, before the passing of that Act, to bury in the Churchyards and Graveyards, that have been since vested in the Representative Church Body, are still entitled to bury therein. I am also of opinion that the right to perform service at burials conferred by the Act 31 and 32 Vic. cap. 103, still exists in the cases where it existed at the time of the passing of the Irish Church Act, although the Graveyard may have been vested in the Representative Church Body since the passing of that Act."

---

Below is given a form of the "Notice" required by the Act of 1868, to be furnished to the Incumbent twenty-four hours before the time intended for the burial; it is in exact accordance with the requirements of the Act. Of course a Notice so formal, is to be used only when a Minister has reason to fear unwillingness to concede his rights. Where the Clergy, or others who have the charge of the Burial ground, are friendly, a less formal Notice will suffice.

It is well to remember that by the Act of 1868 certain "small Churchyards given or purchased for the sole use of persons attending the worship of the" Protestant Episcopal Church, or attached, for the like exclusive use, to recently "erected perpetual cures and District parishes," may, "by the Lord Lieutenant in Council, on application from the Incumbent," be declared exempt from the operation of said Act, and, of course, from any claim of right on the part of a Methodist Minister to conduct a Burial Service therein.

TO THE REVEREND
REV. AND DEAR SIR,
    As the duly appointed Minister of the Methodist Society and Congregation at            whereof the late

was a member, and who at the time of     decease was resident in the parish of                , I beg to give you Notice that it is my intention, at the desire of the friends of said deceased, to attend at      interment, which is fixed to take place in the graveyard of                , on
next, the                , at the hour of       o'clock noon, and there to perform such Burial Service at the grave as is usual and customary at burials of persons belonging to the Methodist Church, provided that there be no celebration catechising, or instruction, already appointed to be held in the Church to which such graveyard belongs, either during the time fixed for such interment, as above, or within half-an-hour before or after the same; and also provided that there be no other Burial Service fixed to be held at the same time and place; and I have to request that if there be any such celebration, catechising, instruction, or Burial Service appointed before you receive this Notice, which would interfere with the Service intended to be held by me, as above mentioned, you will, as required by the undermentioned Act, give me immediate information thereof, in order that I may cause said interment and Service to be deferred to a more convenient hour. And take notice that this intimation is given you pursuant to the third section of the Act 31 and 32 Victoria, chapter 103.

           Yours faithfully,

# INDEX.

# INDEX.

\*₊\* The references are to the numbered paragraphs, except where "page" is mentioned; figures within brackets () refer to sub-paragraphs.

---

Accounts of Circuit Income and Expenditure, 270, 271, 294.
Admission of Members of Society, 4.
Admission into Full Connexion, 97—100.
Additional Ministers, Rules concerning Application for and Appointment of, 299, 300.
Affliction, Grants for, 295 (3, 4).
Appeal in case of Trial of Members, 30, 32.
  ,, in case of Trial of Ministers, 207, 208.
Appointment of Ministers for a third year, 106.
Appointment of Ministers to Circuits on which they had previously travelled, 107.
Army and Royal Navy, Rules relating to work in the, 302—307.
Arrangement of Conference Business, 163.
Arrival of Ministers on New Circuits, 112.
Assessment for Children's Fund, 313 (3).
  ,,   for Supernumerary Ministers' Fund, 321.
  ,,   to be accounted for Quarterly, 267.
Associations, Young Men's, 257, 258,
  ,,   for Home Mission Fund, 280 (2).
Assistant Secretaries of Conference, 178.

## INDEX.

Bands of Hope, 259, 414 (1—14).
Bankruptcy of Members, 13—15.
Baptism, Sacrament of, in the Public Congregation, 49.
    ,,    ,,    Preachers on Trial not to administer, 50.
Baptisms to be Registered, 51.
    ,,    Certificates of, 52, 53.
Bequests for Support of the Ministry, 262.
    ,,    Trustees of, 364.
Burials Law, Provisions of the, page 192.
    ,,    Copy of Notice required by, page 195
    ,,    Opinion of Counsel concerning, page 194.

Candidates for the Ministry, 67—76.
    ,,    ,,    on the List of Reserve, 77—80.
    ,,    ,,    Certificate of Health required from, 76.
    ,,    ,,    at the Methodist College, 81—86.
Capitation Allowance for Wesleyan Troops, Rules concerning, 307.
Chairmen of Districts, Appointment of, 199.
    ,,    ,,    Duties of, 209—213.
    ,,    ,,    Official Expenses of, 287.
Chapels, Permission to erect, enlarge, etc., 332—336.
Chapel Fund, Origin of, 323.
    ,,    General Rules of, 324—330.
    ,,    Grants and Loans from, 329, 331.
Chapel Stewards, Appointment and Duties of, 223, 224.
Chaplaincies and Connexional Offices, Rule concerning appointment to, 110.
Children's Fund, 312, 313.
Circuit Income and Expenditure, 260—269.
Circuit Accounts, 270, 271, 294.
Circuit Schedule Books, 113 (2), 344.
Circuit Stewards, Appointment and Duties of, 227, 228.
Class Meeting, Contributions in, 25, 26.
    ,,    Suggestions concerning, 37—40.
Class Meetings to be maintained, 36.
Committee of Privileges, 192—194.
Conference, The Legal, 143.

Conference, The Legal, Vacancies in, 144, 145.
,,          ,,      Chief Powers of, 146.
,,          ,,      Delegate of, in Ireland, 147, 148.
,,          ,,      Irish Members of, 149.
Conference, The Irish, 150, 178.
Conformity to the World forbidden, 9, 12.
Credentials to Ministers, Rule concerning, 120.

Dancing not to be taught, 9.
Daily Schools, Visitation, Inspection, and Examination of, 377—379.
,,       ,,      Rules as to Management of, 380 (1—10).
Deed of Declaration, or Deed Poll, page 169
Deputations, Home Mission Fund, 280 (3).
,,          Expenses of, 288, 363.
,,          Missionary, 362.
,,          Plan for, 363.
District Chapel Sub-Committee, 333, 352 (3).
District Chapel Secretaries, Appointment and Duties of, 343, 352 (1, 2, 4, 6).
District Education Secretaries, Appointment and Duties of, 365, 375, 376.
District Meetings, Origin and Design of, 195, 196.
,,          Annual, 197—200.
,,          Financial, 201.
,,          Minor, 202—208.
,,          Chairmen of, 199, 209—213.
,,          Secretaries of, 200, 214—217.
,,          Preachers on Trial not to vote at, 197.
Donations on Annuity, 311.
Dress, Simplicity in, recommended, 10.

Education Fund (see General Education Fund).
Education Secretaries, District, 375, 376.
Election to Representative Session of Conference, Rules affecting, 156, 162.
Examination of Candidates, 70, 75.
,,          ,,      Special Committee for, 75.

INDEX. 201

Examination of Preachers on Trial, 89, 93,
,, for Admission into Full Connexion, 98, 99.
,, of Local Preachers, 134.
Exclusion of Members, 29—34.
,, of Ministers, 121—126.

Family Worship enjoined, 60.
,, Directions for, 61.
Fasting, Days of, 59.
Financial District Meeting, 201.
Full Connexion, Admission into, 97, 100.
Furniture, Allowance to Supernumerary Ministers and Ministers Widows for, 309.
Furniture Book to be kept, 276.
Furniture, Grants for, 295 (5, 6).
,, Rules Concerning care of, 277 (1—5).

General Rules of the Methodist Society, 3.
General Committee of Management, 183—191.
General Mission, Rules Relating to the, 301 (1, 6).
General Education Fund, Origin of, 368.
,, ,, General Rules of, 369—374.
Grants from Home Mission Fund (see Home Mission and Contingent Fund).
Glebe Loan Instalments, Payment of, 310.
Governing Body of Methodist College, 390 (1).
,, of Methodist Female Orphan School, 405 (1—5).

Helper, The Twelve Rules of a, 65.
Hibernian Auxiliary to the Wesleyan Methodist Missionary Society—
,, ,, Origin of, 353.
,, ,, Committee of, 354—356.
,, ,, Remittances to Treasurers of, 357.
,, ,, Grants from the Parent Committee, 358.
,, ,, Deputation for, 262, 263.
Home Mission and Contingent Fund—
,, ,, Origin and Design, 278.

Home Mission and Contingent Fund—
,,   ,,   Sources of Income, 279.
,,   ,,   General Rules of Administration, 281—289.
,,   ,,   Grants from, Rules Concerning, 290—294.
,,   ,,   Associations for Support of, 280 (2).
,,   ,,   Deputations for, 280 (3).
,,   ,,   Grants made to Circuits, not to Individual Ministers, 284.
,,   ,,   Time of Payment of Grants, 285.
,,   ,,   Remittances on Account of, 286.
,,   ,,   Contingent Expenses of, 287.
Hymns, Directions concerning use of, 35 (6, 7.)

Investment of Bequests, 262, 364.
Irish Conference, 150.
,,   Constitution of, 151—155.
,,   Rules affecting Elections to, 156—162.
,,   Arrangement of Business of, 163—165.
,,   General Rules of Procedure in, 166—172.
,,   Officers of, 173—178.
Insurance of Trust Property, 348, 349.
Itinerancy, Clause of Deed Poll providing for the, 105.
,,   Rules of Conference concerning the, 106—112.

Junior Married Ministers, Special provision for, 274.
Leader, Business of a, 3 (3), 218.
Leaders, Directions to, 37.
,,   Change of, if unfit, 38.
,,   Appointment of, 219, 220.
Leaders' Meeting, 221.
,,   ,,   Secretary of 226.
Legal Conference, 143—149.
List of Reserve, Candidates on the, 77—80.
Loans from Board of Public Works, 232, 310, 330.
Local Preachers, Rules concerning, 127—142.
Lord's Day, Observance of the, 20—23.
Lord's Supper, Rules concerning the, 54—58.

Lottery Tickets not to be bought or sold, 11.
Love Feasts, 41.

Marriage of Members. 16—19.
,, of Ministers, 101—104.
,, Law, Digest of, Appendix II., page 179.
Means of Grace, 35, 61.
Membership in Methodist Society, Condition of, page 4.
Members, Admission of, 4.
,, Removal of, 5—8.
,, Bankruptcy of, 13—15.
,, Contributions of, 24—28.
,, Trial and Exclusion of, 29—34.
Memorials to Conference, Rules concerning, 171, 233.
Methodism, Origin of, 1.
,, ,, In Ireland, 2.
,, Does not exist for the purposes of party, 66 (11).
Methodist Society, General Rules of the, 3.
Methodist Ministers, Office and Duty of, 63—66.
,, Must not engage in Trade, 66 (1).
,, Should maintain a kind and Catholic spirit, 66 (12).
Methodist College, Origin and Design of, 387—389.
,, Scheme of Management of, 390.
,, Governing Body of, 390 (1).
,, Endowments of, 390 (2).
,, Religious Instruction in, 390 (3).
,, Scholarships in, 390 (5).
,, President, Head Master, and Treasurer of, 390 (6);
,, Theological Department of, 390 (7).
,, Candidates for the Ministry in, 82, 86.
,, Ministers' Sons in, 390 (2).
,, Ministers' Daughters in, 390 (8).
,, M'Arthur Hall in connection with, 390 (9).
,, Conference power of Visitation and Alteration of, 390 (10).
Methodist Orphan Society, 391, 392.
,, Rules as to Admission to Benefit of, 394, 395, 396.
,, Management of, 397, 402.

Methodist Female Orphan School, Origin of, 403, 404.
    ,,    ,,    Scheme of Management of, 405.
    ,    ,,    Resolutions of Conference concerning, 406.
Ministers, Official Relation to Circuits, Termination of, 111.
    ,    Supernumerary, 114—117.
    ,,    Resignation of, 118, 119.
    ,,    Rule concerning Credentials given to, 120.
    ,,    Trial and Exclusion of, 121—126.
Ministers' Residences, Rules concerning, 275—277.
Ministers' Sons' Fund, Origin of, 314.
    ,,    ,,    Rules of Administration of, 315 (1—9).
Ministers' Daughters' Fund, Origin of, 316.
    ,,    ,,    Rules of Administration of, 317 (1—7).
Ministerial Session of Conference, Constitution of, 152.
Ministerial Support, 272—274.
Minor District Meeting, The, 202—208.
Missionary Prayer Meetings, 45.
Missionary Society (see Hibernian Auxiliary).
Missionary Deputations, 362.
    ,,    Plan for, 363.
Mission Schools, Inspection of, 361, 378, (see also Daily Schools).
Moral and Spiritual Report from Dependent Circuits, 289.

National Schools, General Rules concerning, 380.
New Appointments to Office, Rule concerning, 170.
New Classes to be Formed, 39.
New Laws, Rules and Regulations, Rule concerning, 169.
Notice required of any proposed change in Constitution, 167.
Notes of Removal, Members to receive, 5.

Observance of Lord's Day, 20, 23.
Office and Duty of a Methodist Minister, 63—66.
Official relation between a Minister and his Circuit, Termination of, 111.
Official Expenses, 287.
Open-air Preaching, 47.
Ordination of Preachers received into Full Connexion, 100.

# INDEX.

Origin of Methodism, 1.
,, in Ireland, 2.
Original Rule of Contribution, 25.

Pastoral Address to be read to the Society, 43.
Pastoral Visitation enjoined, 64, 66 (3).
Petitions for appointment of Ministers, 106, 108, 109.
Plans of proposed New Erections to be submitted, 335.
Poor's Fund, Stewards of the, 222, 225.
Poll Deed, or Deed of Declaration, Appendix I., page 169.
Prayer Leaders, Appointment of, 245, 247, 248.
Prayer Meetings, 44, 46, 245, 246, 247.
Preachers on Trial, 87—95.
,, Are not to Marry, 96.
,, Behaviour and Studies of are to be inquired into by Superintendent, 113 (1).
President of Conference, Appointment and Powers of, 173.
,, To Decide Doubtful Questions as to Order of Business, 168.
Privileges, Committee of, 192—194.
Procedure, General Rules of, in Conference, 164.
Proportionate Giving, Duty of, 28.
Public Worship, Usual Order of, 35.

Quarterly Meeting, Constitution of, 229.
,, Chairman of the, 230.
Business of the, 231 (1—15).
,, Adjournment of the, 234.
Quarterly Visitation of the Classes, 113 (2).
Quarterly Fast Days, 59.

Raffling forbidden, 11.
Registrar of Deeds, Duties of, 325.
Registering Chapels for Marriage, Appendix II., page 179
Removal of Members, Rules concerning, 5—8.
Removal Expenses, Rule concerning payment of, 308.
Renewal of the Covenant, 48.

Repairs, Rules concerning Grants for, 295 (6, 7).
Representatives to British Conference, Election of, 164.
Representative Session of Conference, Constitution of, 154.
Resignation of Ministers, 118, 119.
Revision of Circuits, Rules concerning, 296—298.
Rules of a Helper, 65.
Rules, General, of Methodist Society, 3.

Sacraments, The, 49—58.
Schedule Book, Circuit, to be kept, 113 (2), 344.
Secretary of Conference, 177.
Secretaries of Districts, Appointment of, 200.
    ,,    Duties of, 214—217.
    ,,    Official Expenses of, 287.
Society Stewards, Appointment and Duties of, 222, 22
Society Meetings, 42, 43.
Stationing Committee, 179—182.
Stipend of Ministers, 273.
Strangers Preaching in our places of Worship, Rule concerning, 113 (6).
Sub-Committee of General Committee of Management, 189—191.
Sunday Collections, Usage in Ireland concerning, 27.
Sunday Schools, 249.
    ,,    Committee of, 250.
    ,,    Officers and Teachers of, 252—254.
    ,,    Catechetical exercises in, 255.
    ,,    Scholars in, 256.
Sunday School Convention, Time of holding, 367.
Sunday School Committee, General, 365.
    ,,    Grant from General Education Fund to, 366.
Superintendent Ministers, 113.
    ,,    Epitome of Duties of, 113 (1—10).
Supernumerary Ministers, 114, 117.
Supernumerary Ministers and Widows, Furniture Allowance, 309.
    ,,    Fund, and Rules of Administration of, 318, 322.
Supplemental List of Elected Representatives, 162.
Support of the Ministry, 24—28.

# INDEX.

Systematic Beneficence, Duty of, 28.

Temperance Committee, 407, 408, 410
,, Associations, 407.
,, Rules concerning Bands of Hope, &c., 414 (1, 14).
,, Secretaries, 411, 413.
Time of Ministers arriving in New Circuits, 112.

Tobacco, Use of, to be avoided, 12.
,, Candidates for the Ministry must not use, 72 (2).
Travelling Expenses of Ministers attending Conference, 287.
Trial and Exclusion of Members, 29—34.
Trial and Exclusion of Ministers, 121—126.
Trustees, Rule concerning Appointment of, 235.
,, Not to receive Grants from Chapel Fund if they violate rules, 339.
Trustees' Meetings, Rules concerning, 236—240.
Trustees of Bequests, 364.
Trust Deeds, Renewal of, 244.
,, Custody of, 342.
Trust Property, Schedules of, 232.
,, Preservation of, 241, 242.
,, Sanction for Outlay on, 243.
,, Settlement of, 340, 341.
,, Management of, 345—347.
,, Insurance of, 348, 349.
,, Legal Proceedings concerning, 350.
,, Sale of, 351.
Twelve Rules of a Helper, 65.

Vice-President of the Irish Conference, 174.
,, Powers and Privileges of, 175.
,, Has charge of the List of Reserve, 77—80, 175.
,, Is *Ex-Officio* Chairman of his District, 199.
,, ,, of Connexional Committees, 175.
,, Provision in case of the death, or continued illness of, 176.
Visitors at Conference Session, Rule concerning, 172.

Watch-Night, 48.
Wesley College, Dublin, Origin of, 381, 382.
　　　"　　Committee of Management of, 383—385
　　　"　　Trustees of, 382, 386.
Widows' Fund (See Supernumerary Fund)
Worldly Conformity forbidden, 9—12.
Worship, Public, Usual Order of, 35.
Worship, Family, 60, 61.

Yearly Collection, 280 (1).
Young Men's Associations, 257, 258.

www.ingramcontent.com/pod-product-compliance
Lightning Source LLC
Chambersburg PA
CBHW031829230426
43669CB00009B/1282